BeesKnees #3:
A Beekeeping Memoir

Volume Three: Days 201 - 300

The Journey of a Beginning Beekeeper

Fran Stewart

BeesKnees #3: A Beekeeping Memoir
Fran Stewart
© 2019

All rights reserved. No part of this book may be used or reproduced in any manner whatsoever without written permission from the author, except by a reviewer who may quote brief passages in a review.

Cover design by Darlene Carter

ISBN: 978-1-951368-03-6

This book was printed in the United States of America.

Published by
My Own Ship Press
PO Box 490153
Lawrenceville GA 30049

myownship@icloud.com
franstewart.com

To my grandchildren, with love
You populate these pages (here and there)
You live in my heart always

Books by Fran Stewart

The Biscuit McKee Mystery Series:

Orange as Marmalade
Yellow as Legal Pads
Green as a Garden Hose
Blue as Blue Jeans
Indigo as an Iris
Violet as an Amethyst
Gray as Ashes

Red as a Rooster
Black as Soot
Pink as a Peony
White as Ice

A Slaying Song Tonight

The Scot Shop Mysteries:

A Wee Murder in My Shop
A Wee Dose of Death
A Wee Homicide in the Hotel

Poetry:

Resolution

For Children:

As Orange As Marmalade/
  Tan naranja como Mermelada
    (a bilingual book)

Non-Fiction:

From The Tip of My Pen: a workbook for writers
BeesKnees #1: A Beekeeping Memoir
BeesKnees #2: A Beekeeping Memoir
BeesKnees #3: A Beekeeping Memoir

Introduction to BeesKnees #3

I'm glad you're still with me!

As I transferred these entries from my blog to this book, I naturally had to re-read every single one of them, not only to update outdated information, but also to check out every hyperlink to be sure it still pointed to the right URL.

I was saddened by how many of those websites no longer existed.

Still I've tried as much as possible to replace the dead links with information that will point you in the right direction. The new hyperlinks are available in the ebook version of these books.

As usual, my thanks to my dear friend Darlene Carter for designing the cover, with that gorgeous photo from Pexels.com. All photographs are from the public domain unless noted otherwise; and all the ridiculously fuzzy ones—thanks for your understanding—are from an old outdated phone camera of mine.

    --Fran
    from my house beside a creek
    on the other side of Hog Mountain GA

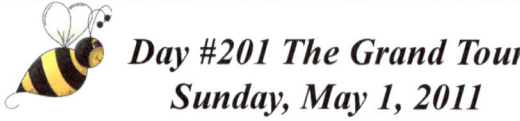
Day #201 The Grand Tour
Sunday, May 1, 2011

It was so much fun Saturday when a friend of mine came by to see the bees. We walked slowly up next to the hive and settled in to watch. It wasn't much of a tour—just two hives on my back deck—but it sure did feel grand.

The ladies were in a fine mood, zipping into the hives with their loads of pollen, all bright yellow in the corbiculae on their back legs. Zipping out again, they launched themselves into the sunlight like tiny racehorses out of the starting gate.

My friend felt as I did—that this was a sacred moment.

BeeAttitude for Day #201: *Blessed are those who see the sacred in the everyday, for they shall hold heaven in their hearts.*

One thing Fran is grateful for right now: *Hugs from all the grandkids at Aiden's soccer game*

Day #202 Answers to the Latest Bee Joke
Monday, May 2, 2011

The question was **"How do you hug a bee?"**
Here are the answers so far:
- From bee-hind - Texas
- Bee-tween the front legs - Minnesota
- On a wing and a bee-rayer (*think WWII song*) - Illinois
- Do it while you sing "I love bee truly" - California
- No matter how you do it, it's beeyootiful - Colorado
- With a dozen legs entwined (if you're another bee) – New York
- With 8 legs entwined (if you're a human BEEing) – same place

You're all winners.

p.s. Thank you, Illinois, for including the explanation!

p.s. #2 Happy Birthday, Veronica!

BeeAttitude for Day #202: *Blessed are those who laugh at themselves, for they shall have good lung power.*

One thing Fran is grateful for right now: *The Atlanta Pen Women Nature Garden at Stone Mountain Park. I love having my name on one of those stones.*

BeesKnees #3: A Beekeeping Memoir

 ## Day #203 First Honey, Sort Of
Tuesday, May 3, 2011

Last week, when I opened the white hive, those bees were building comb that didn't look like anything I'd seen in books, so I put out a call for help. Tommy Bailey, one of the leaders of our beekeepers club, dropped by my house Monday to help me figure out what was going on. I wasn't crazy. The bees had built comb that wasn't attached to the foundation other than at the top. Some of their comb was so deep it infringed on the space needed by the next frame over.

Thank goodness for Tommy's bee-sense. He showed me how to slice off the extra-fat comb so the frames would fit. Then we junked three of the five frames, the ones that had so much messed-up comb they weren't worth saving. This whole operation will set the white hive back a few weeks, but what they build from now on should be better all around. I'll have to keep an eye on it.

We did find an active queen, and there were lots of eggs and larvae and capped brood, so the hive should eventually thrive. At least, I hope so.

Then we checked the yellow hive – and the comb they'd built in there was as bright yellow as the hive itself. I kid you not. BRIGHT yellow. Tommy said he'd never seen anything like that. The thing is, I have this HUGE Tulip Poplar tree in my front yard, and it's been in full bloom for several weeks. Tommy said he guessed that the bees were pulling all their nectar and pollen from there, and that it was turning the wax yellow. Isn't that fun?

Those frames (in the yellow hive) were getting close to being full, so by Thursday I'll probably have to put a second story on the hive, to give them room to expand. Can you believe it? In two weeks, starting from scratch, those sweeties have built themselves a mansion, and peopled it with everything they need not only to survive, but to flourish.

The comb we cut off drained out into a bucket, and I "harvested" about three tablespoons of honey! The rest I left for the bees to rob out and return to the hive. My grandkids thought the honey was delicious. Life is good.

BeeAttitude for Day #203: *Blessed are those who are willing to help others, for they shall go on our gratitude lists.*

One thing Fran is grateful for right now: *The wonderful conversation I had with Tommy.*

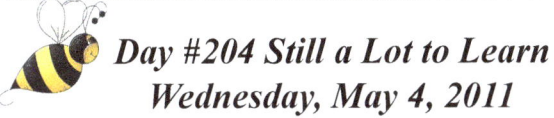

Day #204 Still a Lot to Learn
Wednesday, May 4, 2011

Tuesday I spent some time with my friend Geri, who has a 10-frame hive.

She knew as little about hers as I knew about mine. I'd told her I'd help her open it up for the first check since she brought it home last week.

Guess what? I hadn't a clue whether I was looking at something positive or something negative. So she called Tommy, who—bless him indeed—stopped by and set her mind at rest. It seems the hive is working just fine. All that comb built between the frames is to be expected (I'd thought it was only in MY hive!)

This just goes to prove that I still don't know nearly enough about bees. Of course, Tommy's been around bees for 40 years, since his grandpa and dad had hives. So maybe Geri and I aren't doing too badly with our less-than-a-month of experience…

BeeAttitude for Day #204: *Blessed are those who take time to practice, for they shall gradually get better at what they do.*

One thing Fran is grateful for right now: *My knees that still work*

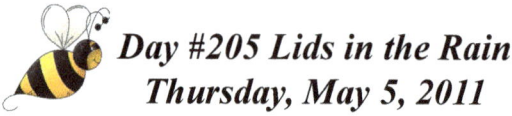

Day #205 Lids in the Rain
Thursday, May 5, 2011

When I took off the feeding jars last Monday after Tommy told me that the hives were doing fine without supplemental feeding, I left the lids in place so there wouldn't be a jar-lid-sized hole in the top of the hives. Each lid, of course, had two or three teeny holes poked into it so the bees could lick the sugar water from underneath.

When it started raining Tuesday night, I fortunately recalled those holes. I grabbed a dry dish towel, some aluminum foil and my big umbrella.

Try crimping aluminum foil around the rim of an upside-down jar lid one-handed.

It doesn't work.

So, I set the umbrella down, sopped up the water sitting in the lids, and secured the aluminum foil.

Inside again, I was soaking wet and thoroughly happy.

What I do for these bees . . .

Next time rain is forecast, I'll replace the hole-y lids with solid ones. In the meantime, I've taken off the aluminum foil so the bees can have a little more ventilation for all that moisture they're fanning out of the nectar. Wouldn't want to slow down their honey-production.

BeeAttitude for Day #205: *Blessed are those who are willing to commit themselves to important causes, for they shall feel good about themselves.*

One thing Fran is grateful for right now: *The breeze coming in through open windows*

Day #206 Come on Over
Friday, May 6, 2011

This afternoon, I'll be adding a second story to my yellow hive. They've done so well in only two and a half weeks, that they've almost filled the first hive body.

I'll also be moving the bees that are in the white hive into a new box, one that I put together myself and stained brown to match the deck. So from now on the white hive will be known as **"the brown hive."** Clear as mud?

If you want to come by and watch the process, give me a call. I have an extra veil I can lend you. You might even catch the *bee-fascination* bug, and want your own hives!

BeeAttitude for Day #206: *Blessed are those who discover new talents, for they shall thrive.*

One thing Fran is grateful for right now: *The HUGE potato plants growing in a garbage can on my deck, thanks to an article in Mother Earth News*

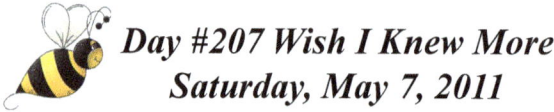

Day #207 Wish I Knew More
Saturday, May 7, 2011

Well, I think I may have another problem, and I'm not sure what to do about it.

It turns out the brown box isn't as deep as the white box or the yellow box. I don't know what happened, because I ordered a "deep hive body," and I guess I assumed it would match the size of the others. I think what I got was a "medium." That's what comes of not knowing enough about what I'd ordered to check it when I picked it up. All those words – deep, medium, and super – were just that. Words. Without the experience of working with the various sized hive units, I simply didn't know what I was doing.

I have a feeling I've squashed the bottom part of the frames against the screened bottom that I spent a lot of time attaching to the bottom of the brown box. I sent off an email to the folks I bought it from, asking them what was up and if there would be a problem for the bees.

Hope I hear back soon . . .

Meanwhile, if this is the worst thing I have to worry about, I'm in pretty good shape. My friend Dauna Coulter, a writer for **Science News @ NASA** lives in Huntsville, Alabama, and went through all that recent hurricane damage.

BeeAttitude for Day #207: *Blessed are those who write about their experiences, for they shall pass on an enduring legacy of memories.*

 Day #208 Sherlock Holmes
Sunday, May 8, 2011

A week or so ago I picked up a copy of *The Adventures of Sherlock Holmes*. I'd read it, of course, decades ago, but I wanted to revisit some favorite stories, particularly "The Speckled Band" and "The Red-Headed League."

Sherlock was always remonstrating about poor Watson's inability to *observe* what he was seeing. He could just as well have been talking about me. Occasionally I've seen a whole flock of bees hovering right outside the entrance to the hive, but because I didn't know what I was looking at, I was as much in the dark as good old Watson. I thought they were just coming and going the way bees do.

Now, however, I've graduated to Sherlock-status. When a brand new baby bee emerges from its cell, the first thing it does, as I've mentioned before, is to turn around and clean out that cell. Once her little wings are dry, though (and this is that vital piece of information I didn't have before), she heads for the front door, flies for the very first time, but only goes out a foot or two where she reverses course and checks out just where her home is. It takes her a while to orient herself completely, and during that time (along with all her sister babies who emerged the same time as she did) she flies back and forth, back and forth, looking at the hive, the setting, any nearby landmarks.

Once she knows indelibly where she belongs, she returns to the hive and takes up her function as a cleaning bee.

Elementary, my dear.

BeeAttitude for Day #208: *Blessed are those who observe what they're seeing, for they shall be filled with insight.*

bee.s. from Fran: Make someone happy—tell a friend about my books!

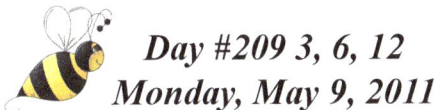 *Day #209 3, 6, 12*
Monday, May 9, 2011

Okay, I finally have it straight.

Here's the beginning of the life cycle of a bee:
- 3 days as an egg
- 6 days as a larva
- 12 days as a pupa

When I check my hives and see eggs present, it means that there was a queen present *at least* 3 days ago. That's a good thing to know if I can't find the queen – and believe me, she's very good at hiding.

In the first three days, there's nothing too much for the nurse bees to do, but as soon as the egg hatches, they start feeding that little critter. After six days, the big bees put a cap of brownish wax over the cell, and wait twelve days for the creature inside to mature into a worker bee, at which point the baby bee starts the next six weeks of her very productive by taking an orienting flight (see yesterday's blog post).

I know I've written about all this before, way back when I was starting this blog and reading everything I could about honeybees, but NOW, now that I'm able to see the workings of the hive, it's all making a lot more sense.

I wish you could join me in a hive check sometime.

BeeAttitude for Day #209: *Blessed are those who read, for that reading shall start them on a lifetime of adventure.*

Day #210 High-Rise Apartments for Apis Mellifera
Tuesday, May 10, 2011

Yippee! My yellow hive now is two stories tall.

Late Monday morning I started the smoker, opened the hive, and saw the most beautiful array of brown-capped brood and white-capped honey. The frames were full enough that I could move the center one up into a second hive body.

I took the time to check each of the frames, and they were all simply beautiful. I didn't spot the queen, but there were loads of eggs and baby bee larvae.

Life doesn't get much better than this. I hope you're cheering along with me.

FRANattitude for Day #210: *Blessed are all the library staff members who treated us Georgia authors like royalty last weekend as we talked with library patrons at the "Barefoot in the Park" Art Festival.*

BeesKnees #3: A Beekeeping Memoir

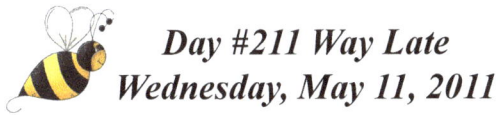 ***Day #211 Way Late***
Wednesday, May 11, 2011

Remember back in October when I was bemoaning the fact that I couldn't figure out how to get the photo files out of my old Nokia phone and into my computer? It wasn't a huge priority for me – obviously – but I finally got around to doing something about it.

I happened to be in OfficeMax about something else altogether, but I mentioned to the sales fellow that I had this phone …

Turns out they don't make the kind of connector I need anymore, but the young man suggested that I get a BlueTooth adapter. "I don't want one of those blue things hanging on my ear," I said with some asperity. "They blink like a runway approach."

"Don't worry, ma'am." I could see that his mama raised him right. I'm always a bit leery, though, when someone starts by saying, "All you have to do is …" No matter how polite the instructor, there is that underlying assumption that I'll know what he's talking about.

Once I got home it took me only about two and a half hours to figure out how to translate his "easy steps" into a working connection.

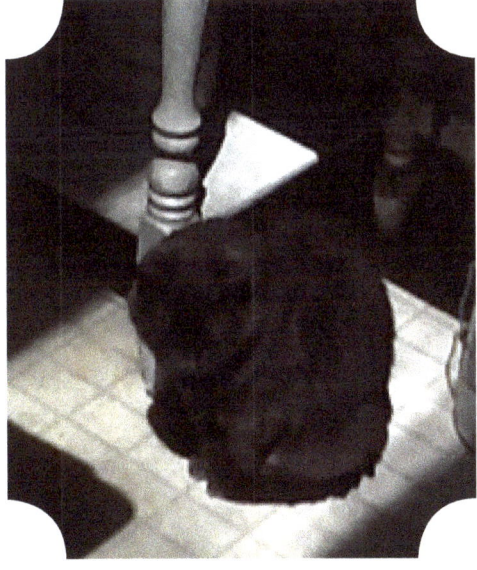

So, now I'll be able to show you actual pictures of my hives. But first, Miss Polly and Daisy wanted to be included. And, of course, you can see the new bee-suit as Daisy tried it on.

BeeAttitude for Day #211: *Blessed are those who keep trying, even when the first time doesn't work, for they shall eventually succeed and feel darn good about themselves. We bees do that when looking for good nectar sources.*

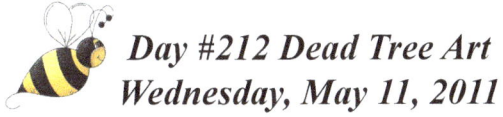 ### Day #212 Dead Tree Art
Wednesday, May 11, 2011

Some time ago I had three dead maples cut down. The resulting light and extra root space has been very good for my tulip poplar tree (and the resultant pollen the bees enjoyed).

I promised you that, when I figured out how to get the pictures out of the camera, I'd show you the starburst patterns formed by the dead channels at the heart of the tree.

Here they are. The first one is an angled cut.

Firewood ready for splitting.

Amazing, eh?

When I look at the beauty in these dead pieces of wood, I can't help but think about my mother, who died 8 years ago today. It was the day after mother's day. My sister and I chose not to have her embalmed, and her dead body was beautiful in much the same way that this wood is beautiful. Years later, when it was time to write *Indigo as an Iris,* I wanted to share this experience with my readers, so I wrote about green funerals and about the gentle look of bodies that are not filled with embalming chemicals.

Now, when I find a dead bee on the deck, I gently tuck it underground, knowing that it will become food for the trees that sustain the bee hive community.

BeeAttitude for Day #212: *Blessed are those who take care of the trees, for they shall enjoy shade, and we bees shall bless those people with honey.*

Day #213 Libraries and Useless Hive Inspections
Friday, May 13, 2011

This paragraph has nothing to do with bees, but I simply have to share a magical moment. On Thursday I walked into the library and was stopped in my tracks when I saw INDIGO AS AN IRIS on the special display of "Staff Picks."

None of my books has ever been there before, at least not in my local Collins Hill Branch. I wanted to whoop and holler, but restrained myself. Instead, I turned to a woman walking nearby and said, "Can I tell you something wonderful?" From her startled expression, I think she might have feared I was going to try to sell her something. A few minutes later, though, I saw her at the checkout counter with ORANGE AS MARMALADE! Now that I have that bluetoothy thing, I can show you the (extremely fuzzy) picture I took.

Now – to the bees. I went into the hives (after the library jaunt), and then realized it's only been three days since I put the second floor on the yellow hive. They've started drawing some comb, but I think it's too early to expect much.

I'm going to leave the hives alone for a solid two weeks before I go in there again. No need to disturb them just because I want some assurance.

I hereby declare that all is well in the hives.

So there! I'm glad that's decided.

BeeAttitude for Day #213: *Blessed are those who leave us "bee," for we bees shall respond with happy buzzing to delight their ears.*

Day #214 Ain't Technology Grand, Folks?
Saturday, May 14, 2011

Thank-you to each of you who contacted me when it looked like I'd disappeared. I truly appreciate your concerns.

Blogger had some sort of problem and stopped all new blog posts sometime in the middle of Wednesday. I'm not sure how long it will take them to post the blogs I wrote for Thursday and Friday, and don't even know for sure that this one will show up on Saturday morning just after midnight Eastern Time.

Hive entrance -- Where'd the bees go?

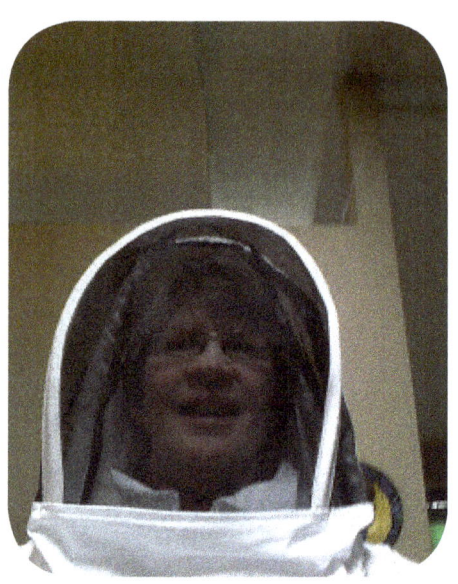

Self-Portrait in the Bee Suit the First Time
I'm not going to worry, though. They'll get through eventually. In the meantime, here are a couple of pictures to brighten your day.

BeeAttitude for Day #214: *Blessed are those who take the time to reach out, for they shall find rest for their worries.*

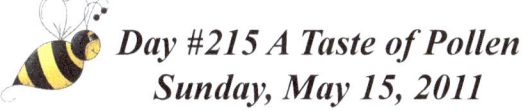 *Day #215 A Taste of Pollen*
Sunday, May 15, 2011

I discovered the most amazing thing! When I pull out the cardboard insert from under the yellow hive, I usually find scraps of the detritus that falls from the hive – mostly small flakes of white wax, little clumps of gray grunge that I think may be propolis, and tiny yellow balls of pollen. This picture isn't the clearest, but it'll give you an idea of what it looks like.

Apparently, it's no simple task to transfer pollen from the corbiculae (the pollen sacs on the back legs of the forager bees) to the house bees who then store it in the comb. They drop some of it, and that falls through the screened bottom onto my cardboard. There is also the occasional bee-bit, a leg, a wing, or a back end that's gotten separated when the clean-out crew moves a dead bee out of the hive.

I decided to take a taste of the yellow stuff. It's SWEET! It tasted like dessert. A very small dessert, since each little puff-ball is only about a sixteenth of an inch (or less) in diameter.

And, before you ask – no, I didn't taste test the bee legs. There's a limit to my adventuresome spirit.

BeeAttitude for Day #215: *Blessed are those who truly pay attention to what they see, for they shall find wonders indeed in and around our hives.*

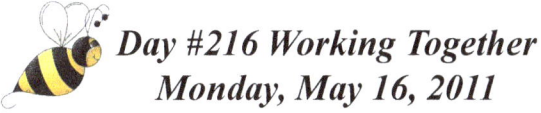 Day #216 Working Together
Monday, May 16, 2011

I love to step out on my deck and sing to my bees. I don't know if they enjoy it as much as I do—I don't even know if bees have ears—but their humming seems to increase while I'm singing. They're such fun to watch, too. I'm always intrigued with how well honeybees work together, each fulfilling her role (or his role—the drones have a part to play as well) without a hitch.

Saturday evening I had a chance to experience something like that when I sang with the Gwinnett Choral Guild. This was a weekend full of concerts – one on Saturday evening and one on Sunday afternoon. The theme was "America Sings" and we performed songs about love, war, peace, people & places, and praise.

I've enjoyed singing with the Guild for years now, and I have to say, we've managed some pretty impressive performances, but Saturday night's concert was one magical *beehive moment* after another. I felt completely attuned to all the other singers and to the marvelously responsive audience. At the center of it all was our director, G. Phillip Shoultz III, who has done wonders with this particular old lady's voice. He can pull music out of me that I didn't know was in there.

Like a beehive, where every bee fulfills her role (whether she's a nurse bee, house bee, guard bee, or forager bee), all of us singers—soprano, alto, tenor, bass—joined to bring alive the music of the spheres. We sang together the way bees work together.

Sitting here now, looking out the bay window at my hives, I can still feel the magic.

BeeAttitude for Day #216: *Blessed are those who buzz mightily, for they shall abound with joy.*

Day #217 Hot Chocolate Taste Test
Tuesday, May 17, 2011

I seem to be in a taste-testing mood. A few days ago, it was pollen. Today it's hot chocolate.

Last week I was at the Gwinnett County Public Library's "Book Bistro" as a visiting author. The library had arranged to have Andre and Latoya Bentley there to serve generous samples of their Organo Gold iced latté. I'm not usually a coffee drinker, but I do admit to guzzling more than my fair share. The day was hot, after all. The coffee is infused with something wonderful called "Ganoderma" that helps strengthen immunity. I'll take all the help I can get.

I brought home a couple of sample packages of their hot chocolate. This is not just any hot chocolate. It has the Ganoderma in it, too. But I wasn't willing just to say "must be good." I did a taste test.

I have two mugs that, other than the color, are pretty much the same. Same weight, same shape. I took the generic hot chocolate mix I keep on hand for my grandchildren and dumped it in the green mug. The Ganoderma hot chocolate mix went into the brown mug. I poured an equal amount of hot water into each and stirred them both.

Then I closed me eyes, sang three of the songs I've memorized for our Gwinnett Choral Guild concerts – "Ashokan Farewell," "Homeward Bound," and the hauntingly beautiful "Prayer of the Children." While I was singing, I moved the cups around. After the first 10 or 15 bars of music, I'd truly forgotten which mug was which.

Keeping my eyes closed, I tasted. Not even close! The Ganoderma chocolate was truly delicious – even more so when compared to that other stuff. It was rich and mellow; no yucky aftertaste, either.

I'll be reporting on a honey taste test once my bees let me rob their hives. I'm no Julia Child, but I do know what tastes good. You can look this up at happybcoffee.com. Tell 'em the bees sent you! *[2019 note:*

This is yet another website that no longer exists, so I removed the link.]

BeeAttitude for Day #217: *Blessed are those who share good news, for good shall bounce right back to them.*

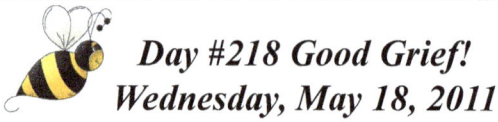

Day #218 Good Grief!
Wednesday, May 18, 2011

Good grief! I've spent hours trying to correct the mess I bought when I got that nuc from a company I will no longer name on-line. It's not just my opinion. The experienced beekeeper who came to help me figure out what was going said that nuc of mine was the sorriest excuse of a nucleus hive he'd ever seen.

A nuc is supposed to have five almost full working frames. Mine had two and a half. And there was a container of roach bait in the bottom. For somebody who wants to do natural beekeeping, this was a setback.

I'm going to make this work, though. Tuesday afternoon I cut out the solid bottom of that nuc box. I'd already cleaned the box as thoroughly as I could, but I went ahead and sanded everything down, and then stapled a screen bottom on it. Whenever the weather's good enough, I'm going to take whatever the bees have created out of the brown (short) box I'd transferred them into, and I'll put them into this clean, screened-bottom box. Then I'll have to pry the screening off the bottom of the brown box and add the brown box to the top of the white one, so I'll finally have two layers, with the deeper one on the bottom.

This means that the **white hive**, which became the **brown hive**, will soon be the **white and brown hive**. I hope you can keep up with this, because I'm getting confused!

BeeAttitude for Day #218: *Blessed are those who take things one step at a time (the way we bees do), for they shall ultimately succeed.*

Day #219 Done! and Settled!
Thursday, May 19, 2011

Wednesday was a full day indeed for two big reasons. I'll start with the second one first.

May 18, 2011 - two layers each

Both hives now have two layers for brood chambers. I opened the brown hive (formerly the white hive) and checked all the frames. Some of the comb they'd built was pretty fat, but it wasn't large enough to attach to the frame next door, so I left it as is.

I saw plenty of eggs, so the queen appears to be well, although as I've mentioned before, she's very good at hiding. There was also a lot of capped brood (the brownish wax-topped cells where the baby bees are growing) and a fair amount of honey (white-capped cells) and pollen (yellowish-brown stuff). And the larvae were plentiful and cute.

I checked on the yellow hive just to be sure, and all seemed well. My smoker went out halfway through this whole operation. Thank goodness I have gentle bees.

Now to the second biggie:

Honey Creek Woodlands Trail

A friend went with me Wednesday morning to Honey Creek Woodlands to meet with the director, Joe Whittaker. Honey Creek is a natural cemetery (also known as a green cemetery) situated on the lovely grounds of the Monastery of the Holy Spirit in Conyers GA, smack dab in the middle of the monastery's 2,200 acres. The cemetery is open for burials from all faiths. I selected a place where eventually (maybe 40 years from now???) I'd like to be buried. And it's all paid for.

If you don't know anything about green funerals or natural cemeteries, you might want to check out the Honey Creek website. Or read my 5th Biscuit McKee mystery, *Indigo as an Iris*, because I have a couple of green funerals in there. Writing about natural burial was my way of helping to educate people about a lovely way to keep pollutants (like embalming fluid / formaldehyde) out of the earth. One acre of a regular cemetery contains enough wood and concrete to build something like forty houses. In natural burial, everything returns to and nourishes the earth.

So – now my kids and grandkids won't have to worry about arranging all that. I know right where I'm going to be planted. It's pretty close to where my friend found a place for herself. You can come visit us both at the same time. But I'm not planning to die any time soon!

BeeAttitude for Day #219: *Blessed are those who plan ahead without freaking out about it, for they shall carry a blessed calmness along with them.*

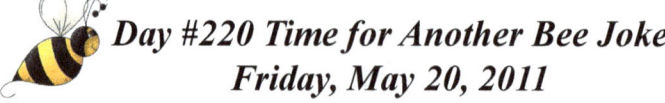 *Day #220 Time for Another Bee Joke*
Friday, May 20, 2011

What do you get when you send a honeybee to the grocery store? Send your answers to me and I'll post them tomorrow.

BeeAttitude for Day #220: *Blessed are those who laugh hard, for they shall exercise their insides.*

 *Day #221 Answers to Yesterday's Bee Joke*
Saturday, May 21, 2011

The question was "What do you get when you send a honeybee to the grocery store." Here are the answers that have come in. I hope you giggle as much as I did!

WY: Chives
TX: A honey of a deal
TX: Honey Nut Cheerios
IL: Beans (bee-ns) and Bee-nanas
GA: Pollen-ta
WY: Green beens
OH: Nectarines

BeeAttitude for Day #221: *Blessed are those who eat fruits and vegetables that we have pollinated, for they shall be healthy indeed.*

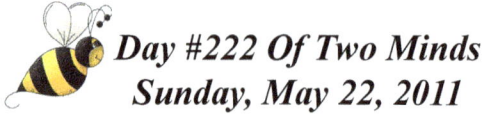# Day #222 Of Two Minds
Sunday, May 22, 2011

I grew up in an Air Force family. We moved so often, that my sister and I can remember what grade we were in when specific events happened, simply by recalling the *place* we were at. Fell down the long staircase – I must have been three because we were living in Tennessee; climbed trees with Phillip Van Stavern and he fell out of a pine and broke his arm – I was five, because we were at Shaw Field in South Carolina; Brownie Scouts with Diane Marie Hart and Ivy McKee – third grade, Sembach Air Base in Germany; learned to hula hoop – must have been fifth grade because we were living on Holmes Drive in Colorado Springs.

People who grew up in one place (like my brother-in-law) often aren't sure what grade they were in when specific events happened. It all runs together smoothly with a common background. They'll remember elementary school times from high school times, of course, but those lazy summers in between school years have a timeless quality for them that military brats almost never had.

I think my bees are like that. They're born, grow up, work, and die in one hive for the six weeks they live. In the winter, worker bees live longer because they're not out wearing their wings off with all the foraging. But still – their entire life is bounded within a five-mile radius of the hive.

Bees that are born into a commercial hive, however, must have a military-brat existence, being hauled from one end of the country to another, following the crops as they blossom at different times in a wave from south to north or from east to west. One week they'll be in the almond groves of California, and the next week in the Midwest for the alfalfa or clover. Avocados here, peach trees there. They cope, of course, but I wonder if they ever wonder what happened to some of their hive-mates that didn't make it back to the hive before the forklift came to load them back on the truck.

I still wonder about Phillip and Ivy and Diane Marie.

BeeAttitude for Day #222: *Blessed are those who keep in touch with friends from childhood, for they shall see the sweep of changes as the people they know mature.*

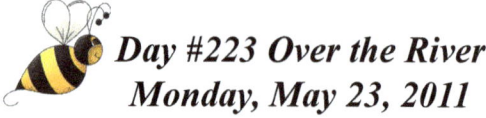

Day #223 Over the River
Monday, May 23, 2011

Yesterday a friend and I went to see *Over the River* at the Aurora Theater in Lawrenceville. The play concerns a young man who's lived all his life in Hoboken, eating every Sunday dinner with both sets of grandparents. When he decides to accept a promotion, which would require a move to Seattle, they try to set him up with a nice girl so he'll get married and stay in Hoboken. The play kept me laughing; even the poignant parts were funny.

As I think about it, though, I'm remembering more poignancy than humor. The play brought up a lot of the reasons why I left home umpty years ago.

Bees don't worry about stuff like that. The only time they "leave home" is when they swarm, and they take grandma (in this case, the mama queen bee) with them. They do it for the health of the hive, not for an impersonal employer. When the hive is too crowded, half of them leave, first making sure that the remaining bees have a couple of queens-in-the-making.

There's no hand wringing where bees are concerned. Of course, bees don't have hands...

BeeAttitude for Day #223: *Blessed are those who know why they do what they do, for they shall have less heartache.*

Day #224 Google Alerts and Online Obituaries
Tuesday, May 24, 2011

I signed up some time ago for *Google Alerts*, so I'd be notified whenever my name crops up online. It's kind of fun, although I must admit I was shocked the first time a Fran Stewart obituary showed up in my inbox.

Another one cropped up yesterday. I take a look at each one of them, just to be sure I haven't been "twained," a word I just invented to refer to Samuel Clemmons' remark about his reported death having been grossly exaggerated. So far, all the dead Frans have been somebody else.

The point of all this is that, glancing through those obits, I've noticed something:
Not one of them was a beekeeper.

I've read that backyard beekeepers as a whole tend to live longer than many other groups of people.
- Maybe that's because beekeepers have to learn to live in tune with nature.
- Maybe it's because people who keep bees are more likely to eat healthily (honey rather than sugar, anyone?)
- Maybe it's because such beekeepers have the music of the hives with them.

Maybe if all these Frans had kept bees, their obits wouldn't have shown up quite so soon.

BeeAttitude for Day #224: *Blessed are those who live in tune with nature, for they shall live longer and enjoy life more.*

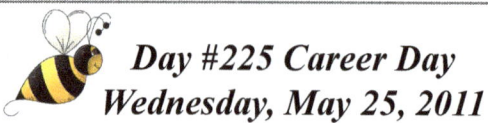
Day #225 Career Day
Wednesday, May 25, 2011

Last week I went to my grandchildren's elementary school to take part in the fifth grade's Career Day. I'd already spoken to each of the fifth grade classes about my life as a writer during the "Writer's Boot Camp" they took part in last month.

This time I spoke to them about beekeeping. I had a set of 12 education cards I'd bought from Brushy Mountain Bee Farm. The bright pictures, each measuring 13" x 18", helped me show:
- the differences between the three types of honeybees (worker, queen, and drone),
- the progression of a developing bee from egg to larva to pupa,
- the hexagonal structure of cells in the comb, and
- the transfer of bee barf from forager bee to house bee.

Everyone got a big kick out of my description of honey as "bee barf," but they agreed it made a lot of sense when I explained that nectar is ingested into a special *honey stomach* by the forager and then transferred to a house bee who then places the nectar (by barfing it up once again) into the cell. All this barfing has a purpose. It mixes the nectar with special enzymes in the bee stomach. Those enzymes help to make honey the super-pure food it is, capable of lasting for thousands of years without rotting.

Yesterday my granddaughter delivered thank-you notes from the children. I thoroughly enjoyed reading them and looking at the pictures they'd drawn as illustrations. Most of the children didn't identify which class they were in, so I'm not sure which particular Jessica drew this picture, but I wanted to share it with you anyway – with thanks to the anonymous Jessica.

This fuzzy stuff is ridiculous, though. I'm just about ready to give up and get a real camera. I wish you could see that the bee on the lower right is saying "Bees Rock!"

BeeAttitude for Day #225: *Blessed are the children, for they shall inherit the hive and shall, hopefully, help it to flourish.*

 ### *Day #226 Food Source / Weed Source*
Thursday, May 26, 2011

There are some folk who would complain if a thistle appeared in their yards.

Not this daughter of Scotland!

I was pleased as could be when this beauty peeked out of (I must admit) a rather scroungy section of my front yard, right next to the driveway. I think it dresses up the area. After all, it's the symbol of my rather prickly ancestors—and their sometimes prickly descendants.

And sometimes not so prickly. Years ago I had a lovely discussion with a Scottish gardener on a hillside in the highlands as we stood beside a perfectly ornamental-looking specimen quite like this beauty.

I have no idea whether or not the bees will see this tall garden addition as a source of nectar or simply food for thought as they fly over it to find something better to eat.

I think it's beautiful. I do plan, however, on cutting it down before it disperses seed! My neighbors put up with an awful lot from me, but there *are* limits to what I can ask of them.

BeeAttitude for Day #226: *Blessed are those with patience and compassion, who live and let live, for they shall be abundantly entertained by the shenanigans of their neighbors.*

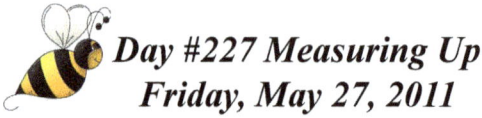
Day #227 Measuring Up
Friday, May 27, 2011

You probably know by now that I'm a voracious reader. And that I love libraries, because they give me a chance to try out all sorts of books that I might not read otherwise.

A week or so ago I picked up *A Measure of Everything: an illustrated guide to the science of measurement,* edited by Christopher Joseph. Don't you wonder how often Christopher was called Joseph in grade school?

At any rate, the book is a compendium of short definitions (from about 3 to maybe 14 lines each) of everything you might ever need to measure. The subjects are grouped according to where they fit in:
- Earth and Life Sciences
- Physical Sciences
- Technology and Leisure

Naturally, I looked up **Bees**. Nothing. Just *becquerel* (a unit of radioactivity) and *bel* (a unit of sound intensity, equal to 10 decibels) on either side of where "bees" ought to have been. I found **blood money**, with its rather gruesome Anglos Saxon definition, and **barn**. Yes, barn. A barn is a unit of area used in particle physics, equal to 100 square femtometers. Aren't you glad I cleared that up?

Then I looked up **Honeybees**. The H's ranged from *haab* (the civil calendar used by the Mayans) to *hysteresis*, which the index said was on page 162, but which actually showed up on 163. I'm glad it wasn't any farther away or I never would have found it and would, therefore, never have known that *hysteresis* is the degree to which a strain depends on the history of all previous stresses as well as the present stress. Uh, right.

Quite by accident, I found **Swarm**, which was right below **Hive**. I should have looked through those H's more carefully. The definition for hive was okay, but I beg to differ with what Mr. Joseph says about a swarm. He should have consulted with a beekeeper before saying that a swarm of bees is led by a queen. Not so. The queen is lured out of the hive by her workers, surrounded, and pretty much forced to go where they decide to go.

Now my trust has been shattered. If he's made a mistake on *swarm*, how will I ever trust him for those essential definitions of **apoapsis**, **kinematic viscosity**, or **rayleigh**?

Sigh!

BeeAttitude for Day #227: *Blessed are those who use words with precision, for they shall, hopefully, be understood.*

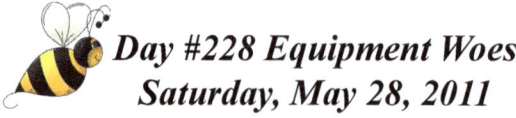
Day #228 Equipment Woes
Saturday, May 28, 2011

I'm beginning to get an inkling of what I've gotten myself into.

Today I unpacked the Honey Filtering System I bought from Brushy Mountain Bee Farm. I now am the proud owner of:

- A food-grade white plastic 5-gallon bucket
- Another just like it, except that it has a hole in the side of it
- A *honey gate* (fancy name for a valve) to screw into the hole
- Three strainers—200, 400, and 600-grade (coarse, medium, and fine-mesh)
- A pail holder, a heavy contraption to stick over the rim of one of the pails so I can balance the other pail at an angle to drain the honey out.
- And a screw-on lid to make it easier to get the 5-gallon bucket open when it's filled with 60 pounds of honey.

The trouble is, if I put the strainers over the bottom bucket, I can't put the pail holder on the edge without piercing the mesh (not a recommended idea). Do I need another bucket?

And I started to wash out the buckets – but I don't have a sink deep enough to hold them. Do I clean them in the bathtub?

No wonder beekeepers build honey houses to hold all their equipment.

Help!

BeeAttitude for Day #228: *Blessed are those who ask questions when they need to, for they shall figure out how to deal with all the honey we will produce.*

 ## Day #229 Six Weeks and the Splendid Table
Sunday, May 29, 2011

I spent some time yesterday idly looking through my Daytimer. *Yes, I keep my schedule on paper. It never runs out of batteries and never has to be plugged in.* As I was browsing around, I did some counting. Today marks the beginning of the seventh week of bees on my back deck.

That means ALL the little worker bees I installed a month and a half ago have reached the end of their 6-week life expectancy. What I'm looking at outside my bay window right now is a whole new crop of bees.

There's not a one of them (except the queen) who remembers the long trip from the bee farm. They don't recall the mistakes I made when I was installing them. They have no idea I was the one who forgot to take the cork out of the queen cage.

What a relief. This is like getting a chance to start over again. Clean slate. New file folder. Next assignment.

Saturday at noon I listened to one of my favorite shows on public radio – The Splendid Table – as they interviewed a beekeeper. We could all hear the bees buzzing in the background. I hope you had a chance to hear it. [*2019 Note:* The link I'd put in the original post is no longer active.]

As I listened, I felt a sense of accomplishment that matched or exceeded almost anything I've ever done in this lifetime. I'm a backyard beekeeper. A member of a select society of people who care enough about this world to do something about it. Eventually, my bees will contribute their honey to my very own *splendid table*.

Life is good.

BeeAttitude for Day #229: *Blessed are those who tell others about us bees, for they shall be lauded for transferring wisdom.*

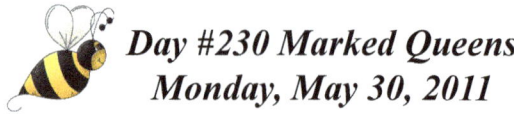
Day #230 Marked Queens
Monday, May 30, 2011

First I have to let you know that my queen is NOT marked.

That said, this is the marvelous system that was devised years ago by people who needed to keep their queens straight.

Professional beekeepers and bee researchers need to keep track of which queen is which. As I've mentioned before, queens can live four or five years, laying anywhere from a thousand to 2,500 eggs every single day during the spring and summer. They may take the winter off, but still, that's a LOT of eggs.

What happens, though, as a queen ages? Her egg laying may taper off so much that the workers feel the health of the hive is endangered. If that happens, you can bet your last honey drop that they're going to replace her by creating a few new queens. Either the newly hatched queen kills off the old one, or the workers *ball* the old queen, suffocating her by enclosing her in a tight cluster of bee-bodies. (Oh dear!)

So, imagine you're a commercial beekeeper opening a five-year-old hive in the spring. The queen you see may be at the end of her life cycle. On the other hand, she may be a brand-new queen. How are you going to tell?

You'll have marked your old queen with a color that indicates which year she began her life. Here are the colors, followed by the ending number of the year in which the queen was hatched:

- White/Gray – 1 or 6
- Yellow – 2 or 7
- Red – 3 or 8.
- Green – 4 or 9.
- Blue – 5 or 0.

I don't plan to mark my queens. I should think a spot of paint would be irritating to them. I've read that the bees don't even notice. **Well, for heaven's sake, how on earth would anybody know what a queen bee is thinking?** I'd like to trust the worker bees to know what's best for their hive. They don't need paint to know who's who.

BeeAttitude for Day #230: *Blessed are those who leave us to our own devices, for we shall grow happily and healthily.*

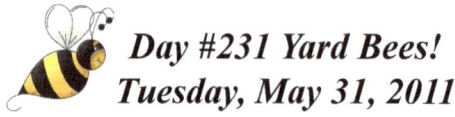 Day #231 Yard Bees!
Tuesday, May 31, 2011

Okay, folks, I'm really excited about this—

I went out to check the mail and found honeybees and bumble bees on the bright orange *Aesclepias* flowers (better known as Butterfly Weed). Here are some of the pics I snapped with my old Nokia phone.

This first picture shows a big old Bumble Bee near some little bitty Honeybees, so you can see the relative sizes.

I'm amazed at how hard they all work to collect nectar. I watched them for quite a while, going from one teeny floret to another, covering them all. And I imagine tomorrow they'll be back again to pull out the newly produced nectar.

And then there was a single honeybee on the biggest thistle flower. I suppose the flower looks huge in this photo, but it's really just under 3 inches across.

I know I didn't plant the thistle. But I left it there beside my driveway hoping the bees would benefit. In this picture, you can see her struggling to plow her way through the thick flower. I hope the nectar she collected was worth all the effort.

BeeAttitude for Day #231: *Blessed are those who plant flowers, for their lives shall be bright.*

Day #232 Another Visit to That Top Bar Hive
Wednesday, June 1, 2011

For a great way to end the month of May, I visited Steve Merritt's top bar hive. You may recall that he was someone I met last October at the very first meeting of the Gwinnett Beekeepers Club, and he offered to show his relatively new top bar hive to anyone who wanted to see it.

I took him up on his offer, but it was so close to the beginning of winter, the bees weren't doing much.

Well, Tuesday I went back and spent time helping him do a hive inspection. We both found out that there are definite disadvantages to the top bar system. Since there isn't any wooden frame around the comb that the bees build, if they goof (or even if the day is just too hot—it was 95 degrees on Tuesday), the weight of the comb is too heavy for the wax attachment on that top bar.

Some of the comb collapsed as Steve lifted it out for the inspection. The good news is that his beautiful, fat-bodied queen most definitely was on one of the combs that stayed in one piece. She was so busy laying eggs, it's a wonder she even knew we were there.

Steve took a lot of pictures of the bees and said he'd email them to me so I can share them with you. I think you'll enjoy them.

I'm also thinking I'm really glad I didn't go with the top bar plan. From now on Steve is going to be shifting his focus to the Warré hives that I wrote about in an earlier blogpost. He already has built five of them.

And—the comb that fell off? I brought a chunk of it home and am planning a homemade bread and comb-honey breakfast! Yummy in the Tummy!

BeeAttitude for Day #232: *Blessed are those who plant trees for shade, for they shall avoid excess air conditioning.*

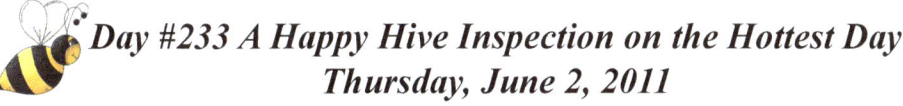 Day #233 A Happy Hive Inspection on the Hottest Day
Thursday, June 2, 2011

Here's a question for you:

How hot is a beekeeper's suit when it's 97 degrees outside?

Next question:

Will Frannie remember to wear a sweatband of some sort the next time she dons her suit?

Thank goodness for the trees behind my deck. If it hadn't been for that shade, I think I would have fried myself on Wednesday afternoon. After my trip to the top bar hive on Tuesday, I decided I'd better go in and check my hives just to be sure the bees weren't cementing the frames together with excess comb.

NOTE: Any comb that's built where the beekeeper doesn't want it is called burr comb. The same way any successful, thriving plant that a gardener doesn't want is called a weed...

There was burr comb aplenty – but I'm pretty sure I caught the problems before they got too bad. I scraped off a couple of chunks of comb that joined one frame in the yellow hive to the one beside it. So far, so good.

I checked 3 of the 5 frames, lifting each one carefully. Didn't see the queen, but there were lots of larvae and capped brood. So I'm pretty sure she's in there somewhere. For some reason I couldn't pick up those two middle frames. Turns out they were joined by a massive chunk of comb right to the tops of the frames beneath them.

I had to pry up the top story and slip my hive tool in to cut the comb. Then and only then could I look at the bottom floor.

Then I went to the white hive. Another story altogether. I'll tell you about it in tomorrow's post.

BeeAttitude for Day #233: *Blessed are those who scrape gently so we bees are protected, for they shall keep us calm.*

Day #234 A Dismal Hive Inspection on the Hottest Day
Friday, June 3, 2011

Yesterday's happy story of the yellow hive turned a bit sour when I opened the white hive (*white on the bottom layer and brown on the top, that is*).

There was practically no comb whatsoever on the second floor. I don't know what's wrong with the girls in that hive. The bottom layer had capped brood and a fair number of larvae, but nobody seemed to be building any comb upstairs. Bees were walking all over the top frames, but no wax to speak of.

I didn't see a queen, but then again, I'm not very good yet at spotting them. There were plenty of worker bees, and nobody had built any queen cells, so I'm hoping all will be well.

I'm pretty sure I won't get any honey at all from that hive this year. I just hope they make enough for them to survive the rest of the year.

And I wish I could speak BEEnglish.

BeeAttitude for Day #234: *Blessed are those who choose alternative energy sources, for they shall help to save our Mother.*

Fran Stewart

 ## Day #235 Honey's Not the Only Sweetest Thing
Saturday, June 4, 2011

Honey is gradually becoming the major source of food sweetness in my life, as I'm trying very hard to eliminate sugar as much as possible, although fudge and molasses cookies are, I must admit, hard for me to avoid. I tried making pumpkin bread (which is really more like cake than bread) using honey, but the result was dismal. Obviously I need some help on how to do the substitution.

A footnote to this: I absolutely refuse to eat anything with aspartame in it. All those addictive diet sodas are slowly killing people who think they're doing themselves good by drinking them. Twenty years ago a chiropractor told me that aspartame helped cause brain tumors. I believe it.

Enough of my soapbox tirade.

I'm still munching away at the piece of comb honey I snatched the other day, and it is sweet, indeed! Food is not the only source of sweetness, though, as evidenced by the craze that's running around the Internet nowadays for "the most irresistibly sweet blog."

I've made the list. Nanette Littlestone, who does double duty as both my editor and my friend, chose my blog as one of two that she deems "irresistibly sweet." I'd encourage you to check her out. Whether you need an editor or simply words of inspiration, check out her website at WordsofPassion.com.

It's a honey of a blog!

BeeAttitude for Day #235: *Blessed are those who see sweetness wherever they look, for they shall be nourished by life itself.*

Day #236 Canadians and the Olympics
Sunday, June 5, 2011

I've had people ask me where I can possibly get my news, since I don't have a TV set. I think that question says more about the asker than it does about me.

But I'll answer it anyway. I read the paper, I listen to Public Radio, and I get daily links to headlines from the Canadian Broadcasting Company.

I've been partial to Canadian news ever since I listened to the Olympics on a Canadian radio station thirty-some-odd years ago when I lived in Vermont. While the Americans were busy bemoaning any loss of a gold medal,
- Bronze? What a disappointment.
- Silver? If only he'd run a little faster. What a shame.

the Canadians cheered *all* their competitors.
- Bronze? Wonderful! What an accomplishment!
- Silver? Our Canadian team worked hard for that.

Gold medals were cheered, too, of course, but the *whole* Canadian team seemed like winners to me—because I absorbed the enthusiasm of those Canadian announcers.

I've stayed true to Canadian news for all these years. Now I'm going to transfer their ideals to my beehives:
- Yellow Hive – Hooray!
- White Hive – You're doing great!

BeeAttitude for Day #236: *Blessed are those who encourage others, for they shall thereby give courage to themselves.*

Day #237 Bees Can't Swim
Monday, June 6, 2011

I've been thinking about swimming lately. It started when I began to wonder if bees could swim. I'm pretty sure the answer is NO.

Every morning I take my (cold) teakettle out to the back deck and refresh the little birdbath bee-watering-place that you can see in this picture. As you can tell, I put lots of rocks and a few water-plants in it, so the bees could crawl out easily if they fell in. Hopefully, though, they'll continue to perch on the edge and take teeny sips. I wouldn't want my girls to drown.

Speaking of drowning, I've spent all my life thinking all the wrong things about what drowning looks like, but recently a writer colleague posted a link on the Sisters in Crime site. **Do you know what the symptoms**

of drowning are? If a friend or a child near you begins to drown, would you recognize it?

I thought I would, but I read the article just out of curiosity.

I was absolutely wrong. I urge you to Google "What drowning looks like" and send the link to friends and family members who live near the water, whether it's a lake, the sea, or a pool.

You just might save a life.

BeeAttitude for Day #237: *Blessed are those who teach, for they shall have purpose in life.*

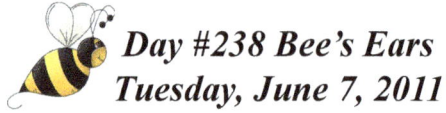
Day #238 Bee's Ears
Tuesday, June 7, 2011

Do bees have ears?

No, that's not the start of a bee joke. I really don't know the answer. I've looked in the various bee books I own, and can't find anything.

At any rate, if they don't have ears, they miss all that lovely buzzing, and all the singing I do when I'm around them.

Or do they miss those things?

When my elderly Miss Polly sat on my lap this morning, I *felt* rather than *heard* her soft purr. Maybe bees are the same. Do they *feel* each other as some sort of ocean wave of vibration? Do they ever imitate each other's sounds?

I don't know the answers. But I like asking the questions.

And I love seeing the early morning sun shining through Miss Polly's ear.

BeeAttitude for Day #238: *Blessed are those who truly listen to what they're hearing, for they shall see the light.*

 ## Day #239 Fun With a Hammer
Wednesday, June 8, 2011

I spent a fair amount of time yesterday wielding a hammer so that I could go from *this*:

to *this*:

I ordered these unassembled honey frames from Mann Lake Ltd., along with skinny nails that were just the right size so I wouldn't split the wood. I have to admit to being somewhat nervous as I tackled the first one, but after that, it was, quite simply, **fun**.

Now, whenever the bees are ready, I'll be able to put the honey supers (the shallow boxes where they store excess honey) on top of the hives. These frames I built will give them a blueprint for where to draw the comb.

Yum, yum!

BeeAttitude for Day #239: *Blessed are the package deliverers, for they shall spread joy, and it will rebound to them as well.*

BeesKnees #3: A Beekeeping Memoir

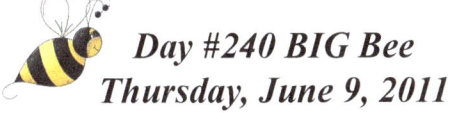 *Day #240 BIG Bee*
Thursday, June 9, 2011

Once upon a time, in the Kingdom of Hog Mountain, in the castle called Harbour House, a woman sat spinning a web of words. Her spinning wheel had been purring for quite some time, matched by the throaty purr of the gray feline on the woman's lap.

"You are being ob-surrrrved," said the feline.

"By whom?" asked the woman, who tended to be grammatically correct, even while spinning.

The answer was a bare breath of sound. "Look—slowly—over your right shoulder."

The woman turned her head a fraction of an inch, and another, and another, and saw the biggest bee she'd ever known.

So she pushed back from her computer (I mean her spinning wheel), whipped out her Nokia, and snapped this photo.

Funny how big five-eighths of an inch can look, eh?

Fran Stewart

I watched this bee for a long time, and was intrigued with how her antennae—I could swear they have a hinge in each of them!—followed me around as I moved my head from one side of the window to the other, as if she were trying to figure me out.

She must have been a fairly young bee, because her tummy was still very fuzzy. About as fuzzy as this photo. My camera isn't sophisticated enough to focus on the foreground.

BeeAttitude for Day #240: *Blessed are those who spin, whether it be yarn or "yarns," for they shall enjoy magic all their lives.*

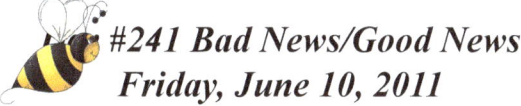 #241 Bad News/Good News
Friday, June 10, 2011

L et me start by proclaiming that my bees didn't do it!

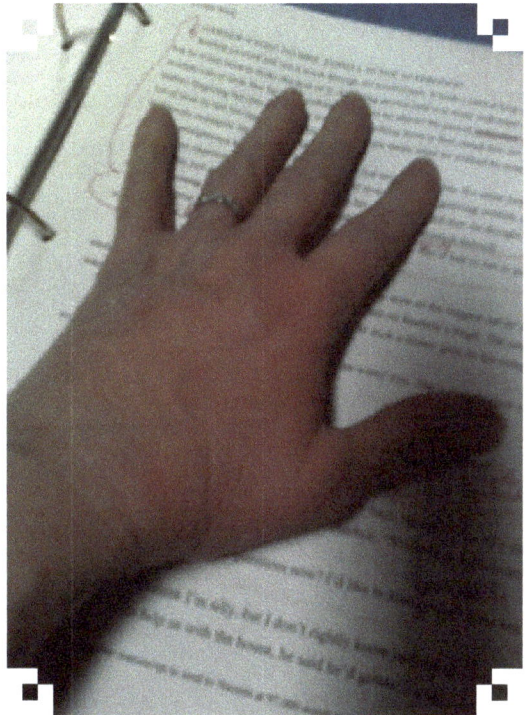

On Wednesday morning I went to my friend Geri's house, at her request, to help her do a hive inspection. Right in the middle of the process, one of her bees stung me on my left hand, on that web between my thumb and my index finger.

Not a problem. I scraped it off, being careful not to squeeze the sac, and kept going. Not half a minute later, another bee stung me in the same location – but on my right hand. A matching set of stings. Once again, I scraped off the little dangling venom sac, and continued helping Geri.

By the time I got home, both hands were red and itchy, but not enough to slow me down.

By Thursday, they were swollen. My normally slim hand was taking on the aspects of a red balloon. So I stopped by the Publix pharmacy and bought an antihistamine. Came home. Took one. But the swelling headed up the inside of my wrist.

I have no idea whether the bee sting or the antihistamine is to blame.

I'll be heading to the doc on Friday, and I'll let you know how it turns out.

Now, the good news: Thursday around noon I checked both my hives (and didn't get stung even once, I'll have you know). I put a honey super on top of the yellow hive, filled with those frames I assembled a few days ago. Talk about good timing! Here it is with all three layers. The other hive is just squeaking along. They still have a lot of comb to draw out before they'll need another layer.

BeeAttitude for Day #241: *Blessed are those who conduct short, efficient meetings, for they shall be loved by the attendees.*

 ### Day #242 Flying High
Saturday, June 11, 2011

For those of you who asked – my hands are much better. They're still swollen, but I can form a loose fist now. The doctor at the Hope Clinic said that I don't appear to be allergic to the antihistamine. The stings were just apparently in a really tender area. And I came home with a prescription for an epi pen. Just in case.

Now on to the exciting news. Let's look at two forms of aerial excellence:

Honeybees Fly

"I know that," you say.

But did you know . . .

People fly, too!

By day **Eli Reiman** is a data base manager. Otherwise, he's a fire-spinner, stilt-walker, juggler, scuba diver, photographer, and now – aerial acrobat. You've seen a lot of his photos *(Yelloideas Photography)* in this blog.

My bees are upside down half the time, too, but I must admit, I've never seen them in bright red…

BeeAttitude for Day #242: *Blessed are those who enjoy what they do, for they shall carry blessings along with them everywhere they go.*

 ## Day #243 Squash Casserole and Beehives
Sunday, June 12, 2011

Rob Alexander, one of the leaders of the **Gwinnett Beekeepers Club**, outdid himself Saturday. Oh, I'm sure he had some help – people who helped haul coolers and food, plates and utensils – but while all of us sat around the pavilion at **Rancho Alegre** and ate ourselves silly, Rob cooked hamburgers, and hotdogs, and bratwurst. My friend Geri and I left before the end, but I imagine he did a great deal of the cleanup afterwards, too.

So,
THANK YOU, ROB!
You get a
Blue Ribbon!

It was a good ole American picnic, with baked beans and potato salad, brownies and fudge, squash casserole (my personal favorite of the afternoon) and coconut cake. Not too many ants. Lots of beehives.

Beehives? At a picnic?

Well, not right there in the pavilion. To check the hives, we had to walk across the field. More than a dozen people at a time gathered around a line of hives, asking questions of **Tommy Bailey** (the other club leader), and learning a lot.

That's what beekeeping is all about – learning.

[Update: If you want to see photos of the picnic, look ahead to Day #262. That's when I finally had some photos taken by someone with a GOOD camera.]

BeeAttitude for Day #243: *Blessed are those who enjoy good conversation as they eat, for they shall have true nourishment.*

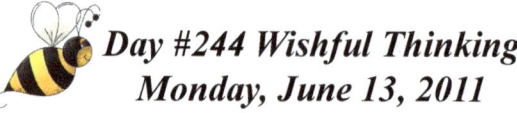
Day #244 Wishful Thinking
Monday, June 13, 2011

Remember last winter when we were all complaining about too much snow?

5 inches on back deck

Now, here it is summer time, and after two solid weeks of days well over 90 degrees, I'm getting wistful.

Come to think of it, though, it would be ideal if we could average the two. I'd vote for some quiet misty mornings.

What's half way between *brrr* and *whew*?

BeeAttitude for Day #244: *Blessed are those who live in the moment the way we bees do, for they shall not waste time complaining.*

Day #245 Shakespeare was a Beekeeper, Right?
Tuesday, June 14, 2011

Scholars have recently determined that William Shakespeare, formerly of Stratford-upon-Avon, was a hobbyist beekeeper. A vital clue to this hitherto unknown facet of his life was revealed after a thorough examination of his writings.

Do you know what that clue was?

BeeAttitude for Day #245: *Blessed are those who read, for their lives shall be rich beyond compare.*

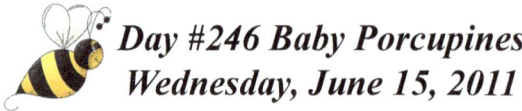 *Day #246 Baby Porcupines*
Wednesday, June 15, 2011

Thanks to the three contestants who entered the "Shakespeare was a Beekeeper" challenge yesterday. Two of them agreed that the best clue was "To bee or not to bee." But then, I'm sure you already thought of that.

Now, on to today's information . . .

I have absolutely no reason to connect porcupines with honeybees, other than ***they're both a bit prickly at times***, but I couldn't resist this photo.

For that matter, I have no idea whether this picture (gleaned, as so many are, from the internet) is really of baby porcupines. [**2019 Note: They're baby hedgehogs.**]

But, aren't they cute?

BeeAttitude for Day #246: *Blessed are those who use their imaginations, for they shall entertain themselves (and us).*

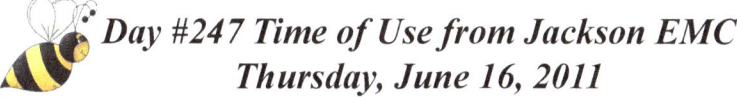 Day #247 Time of Use from Jackson EMC
Thursday, June 16, 2011

Last year I signed up for the Jackson Electric Membership Co-operative's *Time of Use* program. It's their way of encouraging people to avoid using electricity during the peak times – from 3 to 8 p.m. Monday through Friday.

The program runs from June 1st through September 15th. Any electricity used during those peak hours is punitively expensive. But any electricity used any other time (all year long) is quite inexpensive.

They installed a special meter in May of 2010, and I went through the summer using as little electricity as I could. My average bill that summer was $37, while friends and neighbors had bills well over $200.

How did I manage it? At 2:45 every day, I went to the circuit breaker box and turned everything off, except for the breaker that governed the garage door (in case I had to leave on a moment's notice), and the one to the fridge. I had the most peaceful afternoons and early evenings. If I needed light, I lit a candle. If I felt a need to listen to the radio, I played the piano instead. I wrote my books by longhand during those hours and transcribed them (self-editing as I went) during the non-peak hours.

Now, I must admit that if I lived in a sterile subdivision with lollipop trees, I'd have had a hard time with *Time of Use*. But I'm lucky. My house may have been "as is" when I bought it – my flooring may be painted subflooring rather than wall-to-wall carpet, and my furniture (most of it) may be from Goodwill – but, by golly, I love this house. Particularly the deciduous trees that shade the house from the west. So what if I turn off the A/C at 2:45 every weekday afternoon? Those trees are on the job all the time!

So here it is June again, and I'm on *Time of Use* again, blessing those trees every single day.

And when the shade hits the beehives each afternoon, I'll bet the bees are thankful, too!

BeeAttitude for Day #247: *Blessed are those who challenge themselves to do what seems impossible, for they just might surprise themselves.*

BeesKnees #3: A Beekeeping Memoir

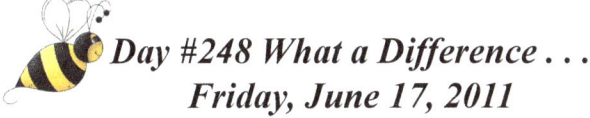

Day #248 What a Difference . . .
Friday, June 17, 2011

I apologize for having spent the last week bemoaning the sorry state of my white hive. All my friends have most likely gotten thoroughly tired of hearing about my poor bees who hadn't done any comb-building as of the last time I checked the hives, one week ago.

To paraphrase an old song, though –

What a difference a week makes, tra-la-la

Thursday morning I called Tommy Bailey, asking if he would stop by sometime soon and help me figure out what was going on in the hives.

He said yes, of course, he'd stop by on Friday, because he's that kind of guy – unfailingly polite and committed to helping inexperienced beekeepers. But he added, as he always has before, each time I've talked with him, "The only way to learn about honeybees is to work the hives yourself. You'll never know what the books are trying to tell you, or what I'm trying to tell you, until you get in there and moves those frames around. Try something, anything. If it works, that's great. If it doesn't, you've just learned something."

As many times as he's said it before, I think this was the first time I *heard* him.

I put down the phone, grabbed my smoker, bee jacket, and hive tool, and headed for the deck.

What I found astonished me. I opened the brown hive first, knowing ahead of time that it was a dismal failure. And guess what I found? Three and a half full frames on the top hive body, with lots of capped brood, lots of larvae, and lots of worker bees.

Sure, some of the frames were stuck to the ones underneath them. I wiggled them loose, scraped off the offending protuberances, and put it all back together. Then I added a super, because it looked like they'd soon need more room.

All this activity going on at a time when beekeepers (including Tommy) are saying, "It's been too dry and too hot, and not much is in bloom now, so don't be surprised if your bees aren't doing much. June is the *down-time*."

Not for *my* girls!

They're as busy as . . . okay I'll say it . . . as bees.

p.s. I called Tommy right back and told him not to bother stopping by. Everything was just fine and dandy at BeesKnees Beekeeping!

BeeAttitude for Day #248: *Blessed are those who provide clean water for us bees, especially on hot days, for they shall be buzzed about in the hive.*

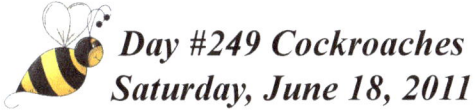
Day #249 Cockroaches
Saturday, June 18, 2011

I apologize in case you've just finished eating breakfast.

Several nights ago I had reason to walk out on the back deck well after dark. There were cockroaches – lots of big ones – scurrying around the deck near the hives. On the railing around the deck, I spotted half a dozen of them scooting out of sight.

So, my question is this: are my bees at risk? Is there a chance the roaches will enter the hives and eat . . . wait a minute . . . **what *do* cockroaches eat?**

I don't have a clue.

One more thing to find out. If you know the answer, do tell me, please.

[**2019 Note:** Nobody cared to answer my question, but I looked it up. Cockroaches are "omnivorous scavengers," which means they'll eat just about anything.]

BeeAttitude for Day #249: *Blessed are those who help their friends, for they shall live in a happy hive.*

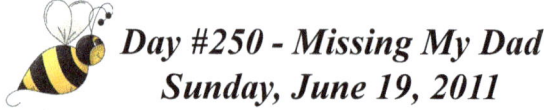
Day #250 - Missing My Dad
Sunday, June 19, 2011

My father was one of those emotionally absent men who cared very much about his family, but who worked very hard to do his job as he saw it, showing his love through that work. I didn't appreciate him (or the work ethic that defined his life) enough as I was growing up, and didn't really get to know him until the last seven years of his life.

I was with him when he died. My sister and I sat on either side of his bed and held his hands as he walked down that long stairway. When he reached the end of it, he took a deep breath and stepped off.

His dying erased any vestige of fear I might have harbored about death. I'm not ready to welcome it—not for a long time—but I know from having seen my dad die, that it doesn't have to be a scary process.

I wanted to share the experience my sister and I had on that March day in 2002, so when I wrote the fifth book in my mystery series, *Indigo as an Iris,* I put in the story a death that looked very much like my dad's. If you read INDIGO, you'll see the loving gentle way he left this life.

I've been thinking about it because, obviously, Father's Day is here, but also because bees from my hives die on a regular, daily basis. I've found their sweet little bodies on the deck, in the planters, and caught in a spider web behind/beside a recirculating fountain. I hope they went as easily as my father.

BeeAttitude for Day #250: *Blessed are those who appreciate their family while they can, for their memories shall be richer.*

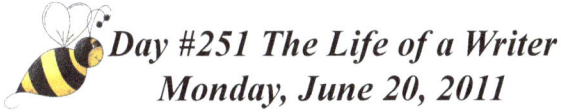
Day #251 The Life of a Writer
Monday, June 20, 2011

In case you didn't know, I've been writing for most of my life, although I never actually published a novel until after the turn of this century. Still, just like in beekeeping, there's always more to learn.

At the suggestion of my good friend Nanette Littlestone (who happens to be my editor as well), I signed up for an online writing class. The instructor, Margie Lawson, is an expert on body language, and she's really good at teaching people how to enliven their prose and freshen up their stale writing.

Not that I think my writing is stale. But still, I learned a LOT from the class. In the book I'm working on now, the town deputy interviews a woman who lives north of Martinsville. He asks her if he can look more closely around her son's room.
- "No." *I wrote in a previous draft.* Mrs. Zapota's lips thinned to a fine line. "He's very particular about his things."

Margie doesn't like thinning lips, and she encouraged all of us (I wasn't the only one) to find a better way to use body language to show what the character felt. This is what I came up with:
- "No." Her lips went from Pillsbury Doughboy to Wicked Witch. "He's very particular about his things."

Fun, huh? I may still change it again – especially if Nanette asks me to – but I'm learning to trust that there will always be things I can learn, and ways I can improve.

Just you wait till I start trying to harvest honey!

BeeAttitude for Day #251: *Blessed are those who call the rain when we need it, for their trees shall be washed and watered.*

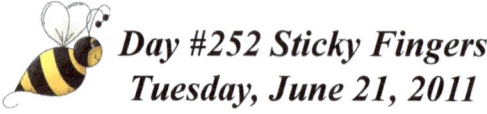

Day #252 Sticky Fingers
Tuesday, June 21, 2011

I love having this little phone camera. The last time I did a hive inspection, I found myself picking up a frame and then having a hard time putting it down again. Or rather, I could put it down, but I couldn't un-stick my fingers from it.

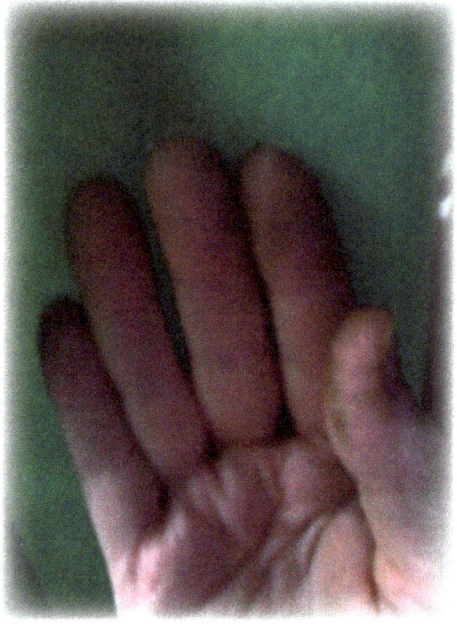

I took this (fuzzy) picture so you can see the brownish-yellow propolis all over my fingers. After I took the picture, of course, I had to clean the propolis scrum off my phone. A combination of rubbing alcohol and elbow grease is about the only thing I've found that works.

BeeAttitude for Day #252: *Blessed are those who aren't afraid of getting dirty, for they shall have many adventures.*

Day #253 It's Raining Thistle Seeds in the Living Room!
Wednesday, June 22, 2011

Remember blowing dandelion seeds all across the lawn when you were a kid?

I certainly have enough dandelions in my yard for both the bees (when the yellow flowers bloom) and the grandchildren (when the seed heads form).

But this year, as I've told you, I've had some **thistle plants** crop up in convenient places (i.e. NOT where I walk). Check back through the blog entries for pictures of the bright purple blossoms *(Day #226—May 26th and Day #231—May 31st)* if you missed them the first time.

As the blossoms go to seed, I bring the stalks inside. Naturally, as they dry out, they pop open. That was a real winner when the grandkids were here last week. They pulled seeds out of the thistle heads, collected them in plastic containers, and . . .

threw them into

the air!

Despite the fact that we'd spread a sheet over the rug, those seeds went everywhere.

BeesKnees #3: A Beekeeping Memoir

© 2011 Fran Stewart

© 2011 Fran Stewart

They looked like stars in the sunlight slanting through the skylights. And like halos on Savannah and Aiden's hair!

BeeAttitude for Day #253: *Blessed are the Grannies, for they shall open brave worlds for their grandchildren.*

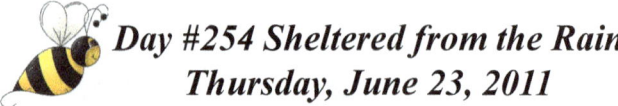

Day #254 Sheltered from the Rain
Thursday, June 23, 2011

We had a driving rainstorm on Wednesday, and I could see clusters of bees hanging beneath the screen on the bottom of the hive, each bee attached by at least four legs to other bees above and below. I tried to get a picture of them (before it started to rain), but there were too many shadows.

I have to wonder, though, if the bees at the top end up with joint problems. After all, having a couple of hundred sisters hanging on HAS to add up to a lot of weight.

Add the 99% Georgia humidity to that equation, and I must give my honeybees a blue ribbon for strength and endurance.

BeeAttitude for Day #254: *Blessed are those who lend a leg to their sisters, for they shall help to form a living sculpture.*

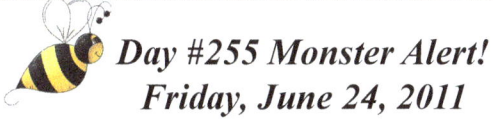

Day #255 Monster Alert!
Friday, June 24, 2011

Remember the picture of the lovely little birdbath I set up for the bees? I filled it with rocks so they'd have an easy way to get to the water.

Now, do you also remember I said I'd put in a rain barrel two weeks ago?

Well, it turns out the rain barrel LEAKS, right across my driveway. For the past week I haven't seen a single bee at the birdbath, but they are ecstatic about the puddles in the drive. *"Water! Water!"* I can practically hear them singing as they zoom around.

The trouble is – now when I back out of my garage, I worry that I might run over some bees. Maybe I could put up a sign . . .

BEWARE: Big Moving Metal Monster!
If you see it, fly away until it leaves!

How would that translate into BEEnglish?

BeeAttitude for Day #255: *Blessed are those who drive carefully, for they shall save their own lives, as well as ours.*

 ## *Day #256 Hive Inspection Yesterday*
Saturday, June 25, 2011

I'm feeling a little bit sad, and I'd like to share the reason with you.

Yesterday I opened both hives to see how much comb the bees had built in the honey supers.

None. Nada. Nuttin. Nope.

I had to accept the fact that I probably won't get any honey for myself and my friends this season. I know. I know. I've been saying all along that if I didn't get any honey the first year, it wouldn't matter. After all, beekeepers are supposed to take the *excess* only. The bees need enough honey and pollen stores to make it through the winter. *[Yes, I agree. It's hard to think of winter when it's 95 degrees outside.]*

Still, there's always been that glimmer of hope. Why else would I order a honey-filtering kit from Brushy Mountain Bee Farm? Why else would I invest in all those unassembled super frames? Why else would I start an Excel spreadsheet of people to give honey to? Why else would I have TWO SHELVES of glass jars stockpiled in my garage?

Why indeed?

As I saw the dismal result of my experiment with the open, top-bar-style supers, I decided my bees couldn't figure out how to build comb there, so I replaced the frames with some plastic-foundation supers. That way my girls will have a template to draw out their comb. I'll feel happy if they can fill it so they'll be ready for winter.

Yes – I'll feel happy about that. But I'm feeling sad about the honey I won't have for me and for you.

BeeAttitude for Day #256: *Blessed are those who change course when circumstances require it. We bees do that, and we eventually find very good flowers as a result.*

Fran Stewart

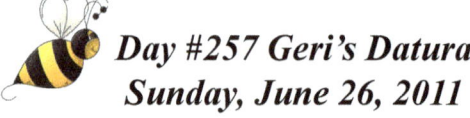

Day #257 Geri's Datura
Sunday, June 26, 2011

I've talked before about my friend Geri Taran. She founded the Georgia Writers Association and headed it up until it was taken over by Kennesaw State University. Geri's had an interesting *(understatement alert!)* life for sure. And she used to keep bees years ago. Once I started getting into beekeeping, Geri decided to take it back up again.

© 2019 University of Wisconsin Master Gardener Program

The last time I visited her, she showed me a datura the birds or squirrels or somebody like that had planted in her yard. The thing's three feet tall now. Datura (also called Angel's Trumpet) is poisonous, as I hope you realize. I found out about lots of poisonous plants when I was researching *Yellow as Legal Pads,* the second of my mysteries. I bought *Deadly Doses: a Writer's Guide to Poisons* by Serita Deborah Stevens. Fascinating. For a mystery writer, that is.

But now I've found out that bees are usually smart enough to avoid plants that have toxic nectar. Good thing. These flowers are so inviting, I should think the bees would have a hard time ignoring them. I took two pictures – one of the flower bud just as it's beginning to unfurl, and one of the blooming beauty (which, by the way, is about 10 inches long!)

[2019 note: my flower bud picture was so outrageously fuzzy, I decided to replace it this time around with these images from the University of Wisconsin.]

Here's the bloom. My camera made it look purple, but it's really a bright white.

HAPPY BIRTHDAY, GERI!

BeeAttitude for Day #257: *Blessed are those who let surprise plants thrive, for they shall be rewarded with beauty, rather like Fran's thistle flowers.*

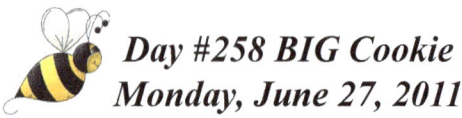 *Day #258 BIG Cookie*
Monday, June 27, 2011

Okay. This has nothing whatsoever to do with bees.

Last Monday my grandkids were here, and we decided to make Molasses Chewies. Savannah asked, "why couldn't we make just one big cookie?"

Why not?

There was a great deal of suspense involved—will the dough expand enough to drip over the edges of the cookie sheet? Will we be able to slide the end result off the cookie sheet?

The answer to both questions turned out to be "NO."

So we decorated the result and took pictures. (Someone said she thought the face looks like the Scarecrow in The Wizard of Oz.)

And we ate right off the cookie sheet. **Yum!**

BeeAttitude for Day #258: *Blessed are those who are open to unexpected ways of doing things, for they shall be pleasantly surprised.*

BeesKnees #3: A Beekeeping Memoir

Day #259 Fresh Eggs and Green Beans
Tuesday, June 28, 2011

I'd be willing to bet that people who keep bees as a backyard hobby are the sorts of people who:
- have a vegetable garden
- buy food at farmer's markets, and
- conserve water as much as possible. I made two out of three on that list.

If you recall those blog posts of mine months ago where I gushed on and on about the veggie garden I was putting in for the bees and for me—fresh lettuce! great beets! crunchy carrots! zesty radishes!—you'll probably assume that *item a* is high on my list of priorities.

My garden, other than a whole bunch of fresh lettuce early in the spring, has been a dismal failure, though. I think it's time to admit it.

I'm okay with shrubs and trees and perennials, as long as they don't have to be pruned, fiddled with, or cosseted.

I'm reminded of a garden I started in Vermont way back in what seems like another lifetime. My dad could grow a garden anywhere, and I've always had this feeling that I ought to be able to as well. One of my dismal failures in Vermont was **cucumbers**. I don't to this day know what I did wrong. I only know that a patient at the family dental practice where I worked at the time was bemoaning his garden's lack of success. "Thank God for cucumbers," he said, adding, "Of course, any fool can grow cucumbers."

This fool couldn't, but I didn't admit it to him.

From now on, all my veggies (except maybe some lettuce and green beans) will come from farmers markets. I love ordering from my local co-op each weekend and picking up my goodies on Tuesdays at a nearby farm. The local farmers

in their network really know how to grow good stuff. And I get to pick and choose exactly how much or how many I want of each item.

I do have one ongoing gardening success. I planted five Kentucky Wonder bean seeds in the early spring. Three of them came up. Now, each morning, I step outside my front door and harvest five or six beans, which is just enough for me to cook in my oatmeal or mix into my scrambled eggs.

And speaking of eggs, my neighbor Janet,
the one who bakes such wonderful bread,
gave me eggs from her sister's hens.
Some of them were blue, and here's
the picture to prove it.

Next year (except for the lettuce and the green beans), I'm planting buckwheat. The bees will love the flowers, and I'll love the honey they make from it. I hope it grows better than those cucumbers.

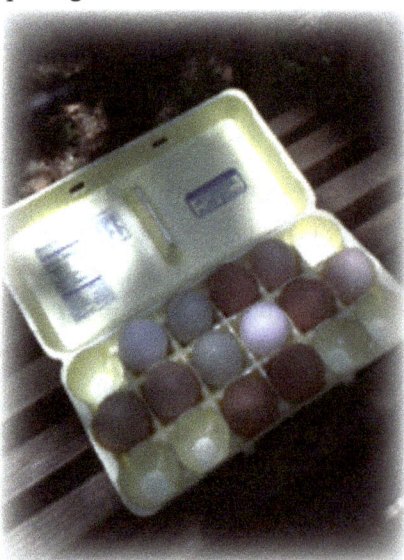

BeeAttitude for Day #259: *Blessed are those who know how to do what they do and who do it well, for they shall be recompensed accordingly.*

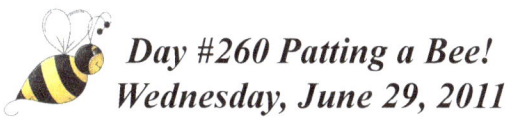 Day #260 Patting a Bee! Wednesday, June 29, 2011

After the last hive inspection, as I gathered up all my paraphernalia, I noticed a single bee sitting quietly on top of the yellow hive.

I couldn't resist the temptation. I patted a bee!

BeeAttitude for Day #260: *Blessed are those who treat us gently, for we shall respond in kind.*

After a little while, she flew off to rejoin her friends, and I floated into the house to write this blog post.

Day #261 Free Plants and the Arbor Foundation
Thursday, June 30, 2011

Speaking of birds, I've thoroughly enjoyed the trees my friend Millie gave me when I bought this house six (seven?) years ago. They came (little more than long sticks) from the Arbor Foundation, but now they're 8 or 10 feet tall. One, a golden rain tree, is a favorite perching place for the birds as they wait their turn at the feeding stations.

It's turned out to be a favorite of the bees, too, with its airy yellow blooms. There are three of my bees and a couple of darker neighborhood bees on this branch. Bumblebees like the flowers too.

And the birds planted a whole patch of sunflowers from leftover seeds they dropped. Here's one sporting a bumblebee and a couple of buzzy little friends.

Three or four years ago, a neighbor said they were taking out a bunch of flowers – did I want any? Sure! So I now have a patch of triple-fringed daylily that the bees have been visiting religiously. There are four bees on this one, even though all you can see is the big guy.

And, finally, my very first crop of blueberries. These plants weren't free, but they did come from the Gwinnett County Extension Service last March. Oops! The picture isn't of the whole first crop. I already ate quite a bit of it. These I saved for breakfast tomorrow.

By the way, did you hear about the canary that caught a case of the chirpies?
Are you ready for this?
The vet said it was tweetable!

BeeAttitude for Day #261: *Blessed are those who see the beauty in cast-offs, for they shall discover wonders.*

Day #262 Bee Club Picnic & the Declaration of Independence
Friday, July 1, 2011

Every Fourth of July, first thing in the morning, for the past thirty years or so, I've read the entire Declaration of Independence (which is about 28 times more than most Americans have read that document). Then, spaced out over the rest of the day, I read the Constitution—the whole blinkin' thing!—(which is 30 times more than most Americans have read it).

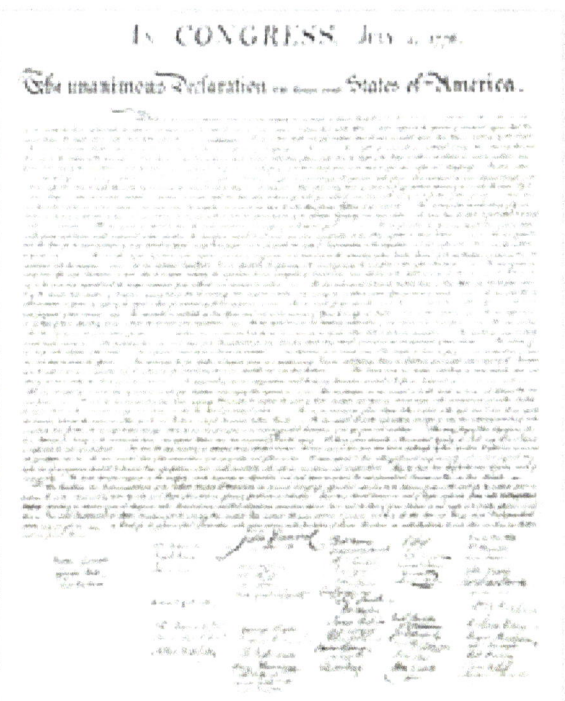

This year, I challenge you to go to www.archives.gov/exhibits/charters/declaration.html and get your own copy to read. It'll give you an idea of what the fireworks are all about.

Ain't technology grand?

Now, on to bees...

With the holiday coming up, a time when so many families go on picnics, I thought I'd show you what the Gwinnet Beekeepers Club does at picnics.

We inspect Bee Hives, of course!

These pictures come from the June picnic/meeting. They were taken by Terri Tattan, a relatively new member. She won the raffle for a 10-frame hive that had been donated by HomePort in Dacula.

BeeAttitude for Day #262: *Blessed are those who include us bees whenthey play, for they shall learn and learn and learn*

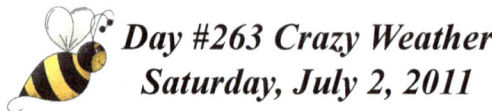
Day #263 Crazy Weather
Saturday, July 2, 2011

Such sheets of fire, such bursts of horrid thunder,
Such groans of roaring wind and rain, I never
Remember to have heard; man's nature cannot carry
The affliction nor the fear ... from Shakespeare's <u>Tragedy of King Lear</u>

Shakespeare wrote these words for the Earl of Kent. We wonder the same thing, though, don't we?

One of my favorite science writers, Dauna Coulter, whom I've mentioned before in this blog, started a recent NASA Science News article by quoting these lines from *King Lear*.

Then, she underpinned that classy start with an astonishingly clear explanation of why we have such crazy weather patterns going on. It's all about "La Nada," a weather pattern that happens every few years.

So, what does this have to do with bees?

They have to put up with the weather even more than we humans do. They don't have air conditioning or umbrellas or tornado shelters. Despite that, they don't complain about the weather.

I'll take that back. Any backyard beekeeper can attest to the fact that bees get grumpy when the wind comes up on a cloudy day.

And who knows what they're conveying to each other when they're all stuck in the hive on a tempest-tossed day full of *such groans of roaring wind and rain*? Maybe that's where Shakespeare got his inspiration.

BeeAttitude for Day #263: *Blessed are those who write well, for their writings shall be loved, and shall give them a special kind of immortality.*

Happy Birthday, Eli!

Day #264 Birds Get Scared—But Bees Don't Care
Sunday, July 3, 2011

There is something infinitely relaxing about bees that I simply don't experience with the dozens of birds who beautify my yard with their myriad colors and songs and flitterings.

You see, even though I've been feeding these birds in this yard ever since I moved into this house seven years ago, they still startle *every* time I open the front door. And they used to do it every time I moved a curtain or walked past a window—until I got smart and installed energy-film on the windows. I hadn't realized it when I bought the stuff, but not only does the film block out a lot of heat, it gives a mirrored look to the outside of the windows, so the birds can't see inside!

That means I can stand there and watch the birds without their knowing I'm observing them. So they don't go careening away. That's good. But as soon as I open the front door, look out! They scatter as if I were stalking them.

Now, I don't mind that, not really. It's a survival instinct.

Fine.

But it's not very relaxing.

Bees, on the other hand, couldn't care less if I open doors, stand at windows, fling back the curtains. I can walk right up to their hives (as long as I don't flail my arms around) or perch myself in a chair nearby (as long as I don't sit on a little bee body), and they don't mind.

Ahhh!!! It's so lovely to be trusted.

BeeAttitude for Day #264: *Blessed are those who trust, for they shall be peaceful.*

Fran Stewart

Day #265 A Ghost Story from Doug
Monday, July 4, 2011

My friend Doug Gazlay, pianist and DJ extraordinaire, puts out a weekly humorous thought. I subscribed to it recently, and the first one that came said:

==========

ROCKING GHOST STORY (by Doug Gazlay)

The other day, while I was exercising, I gazed out the window just in time to see the hammock begin to swing, rocking back and forth.

"Must be windy," I thought. Then I realized the trees were deathly still! Yikes!

Looked again at the swing. Still eerily rocking back and forth, as if someone were on the swing, having a grand old time in the cool morning air! Yikes!

I started wondering who might have died in the back yard and come back to enjoy a visit!

My mind went wild.

Just as paranoia was about to take over, I realized I had left my dog outside and she was scratching her rear end on the swing (out of view, of course). Mystery solved!

==========

Thanks for letting me share the laugh, Doug. I hope your Independence Day is full of fun and absolutely safe.

Now I'm headed off to read the Declaration of Independence...

BeeAttitude for Day #265: *Blessed are those who provide water for us bees on hot days, for we shall buzz happily and mightily for them.*

Day #266 Mouse Problems
Tuesday, July 5, 2011

The other day I took a look at the cardboard piece I have under the hive. It's there to catch the pollen the bees drop through the screened hive bottom.

I hadn't cleaned it off for a couple of days (since I have enough pollen in my fridge to fuel a biplane), and I think not cleaning it each day might have been a mistake. A mouse seems to have found a new restaurant. Pollen Place, I think it's called, with a bit of a Mediterranean flair.

As you can see, Ms. Mouse has been going to town, although why she'd chew cardboard when she can have pure pollen is more than I can guess.

I've ditched the cardboard for a while, which means the pollen is piling up on the cinder block, just waiting for Ms. Mouse to appear at midnight. If I could convince the fuzzies to move, I'd be able to get a little brush under the hive to clean off the cinder block.

They never tell you things like this in beekeeping 101.

BeeAttitude for Day #266: *Blessed are those who bumble along, for they shall eventually get somewhere.*

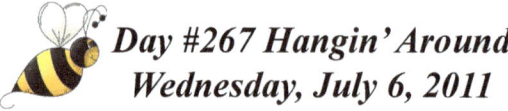
Day #267 Hangin' Around
Wednesday, July 6, 2011

What have I been doing lately? Watching …

goldfinches on the feeder and

Daisy on the kitchen cabinet, and

honeybees on the hive…

What a good day for just hangin' around.

So why have I been I sitting here editing a doctoral dissertation for somebody?

"…because she's paying you to do something you love doing…"

Oh! Right! Thanks for the reminder.

Okay, so now I, too, am hangin' around—editing, and enjoying it thoroughly. Anyway, it's cooler inside here than it is out there where the bees and the birds are.

BeeAttitude for Day #267: *Blessed are those who do work they love, for they shall hang around happily.*

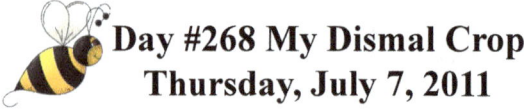 Day #268 My Dismal Crop
Thursday, July 7, 2011

This is embarrassing.

I know I've told you I found out I'm no vegetable gardener. But yesterday I decided to harvest my beets. I'd planted the seeds way back when; all the directions said it was the right time. And I planted them at the prescribed depth.

Here's what I got. That's not a dinner plate, by the way. It's a teensy-weensy salad plate, which will give you an idea of the relative size of those two miniscule specimens.

I left a few of them, just as pathetic-looking as these two, out there. I'll check the others in a month or two and let you know if there's any progress. Maybe a miracle will happen and they'll grow big and fat and scrumptious. But I'm not going to hold my breath waiting for it to happen.

But boy, can I grow thistles! Here's the latest crop, still blooming out by the driveway. I've harvesting more than a dozen seed heads so far, and, as you can see, there are still plenty to go.

BeeAttitude for Day #268: *Blessed are those who know when to give up, for they shall save themselves countless heartaches.*

#269 What Are They Looking At?
Friday, July 8, 2011

I can't figure out these bees. Sometimes they do the darndest things, and leave me wondering at my wealth of ignorance.

I spotted this lump of bees on the decking right below the entrance to the yellow hive. They were there, buzzing mightily, for about an hour. And then they were gone, back to doing whatever bees do.

I got as close as I dared. If I get too close, their buzz volume goes up by about 200%. I couldn't see anything unusual—other than this congregation who seemed to be there for no reason whatsoever.

But they were mighty busy about it.

Wish I spoke BEEnglish, so I could ask them what's up…

BeeAttitude for Day #269: *Blessed are those who speak more than one language, for they shall see the world from a richer perspective.*

Day #270 Time for Another Bee Joke!
Saturday, July 9, 2011

If a bee works in **an ice cream parlor**, what will she put on the menu?

Send your answers to me or post them in the comment section.

BeeAttitude for Day #270: *Blessed are those who laugh hard every day, for their lungs shall be exercised.*

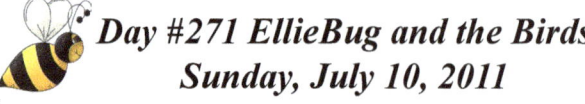
Day #271 EllieBug and the Birds
Sunday, July 10, 2011

I finally got a clear picture (well, relatively clear, considering it's my little Nokia phone) of the goldfinches. You'll have to believe me -- they are BRIGHT yellow.

I got home yesterday after 3 p.m., so I couldn't put the car in the garage—remember, I told you about the Jackson Electric "Time of Use" program, where any electricity I use between 3 and 8 p.m. weekdays during the summer is outrageously expensive. So, I didn't want to use the garage door opener.

Ellie Bug with her yellow spots in the background here (seen through a screen of foliage) sort of mirrors the bright yellow of the goldfinches.

BeeAttitude for Day #271: *Blessed are those who match their cars to their birds (and to us, the golden honeybees), for they shall always be color-coordinated.*

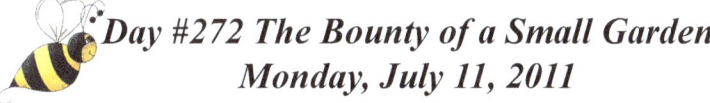 ## Day #272 The Bounty of a Small Garden
Monday, July 11, 2011

Okay. I apologize for all the complaining I've done recently about my failed garden.

You see, there's an incredible bounty in the few veggies I have that DO thrive under my benign neglect.

Here's a breakfast plate, just waiting for scrambled eggs.

And then there's the first gladiola branch.

Life is, indeed, very good.

BeeAttitude for Day #272: *Blessed are those who keep in touch with friends, for they shall stretch their smile muscles.*

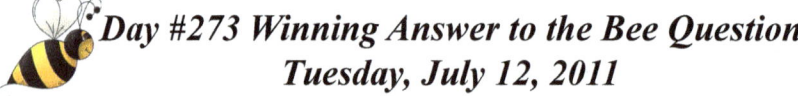 Day #273 Winning Answer to the Bee Question
Tuesday, July 12, 2011

The question was: **If a bee ran an ice cream shop, what would she serve?**

The winning answer, from Maggie in Tennessee: **Nectar**ine Splits, of course!

Thanks, Maggie! Glad you enjoy the blog.

BeeAttitude for Day #273: *Blessed are those who give us a twig to help us out of water and who blow on us gently to dry our wings, for they shall be rewarded with our happy flight.*

BeesKnees #3: A Beekeeping Memoir

Day #274 Elegy on a Country Bookstore
Wednesday, July 13, 2011

Honeybees are in trouble. Everybody knows that. But **there is at least one thing we can do about it**. We can stop buying mass-produced honey. **Most of the honey that people buy in supermarkets has been heated, filtered, and—in some cases—has had other products (such as cane sugar) added to it.** We can pay a little more to buy from local beekeepers. And don't argue that you can't find one. They're around. It may be a little less convenient than pulling a honey jar off a grocery store shelf, but the power of the marketplace is impressive.

I just learned of the passing of one of my favorite bookstores. I met its owner, Melinda Cowan, when I attended a booksellers' convention the year my first mystery was published. Melinda was one of the people to whom I gave a complimentary copy of *Orange as Marmalade*. The following year, when *Yellow as Legal Pads* came out, I did a wildly successful book signing at Cowan's Book Nook. Melinda's enthusiasm for my writing steered customers in my direction. Since then, the Book Nook has hosted the launch of every single one of my books. And I've driven the ninety or so miles up there for book-signings at least three times each year. But that store has folded.

Bookstores, like honeybees, are in trouble. Everybody knows that. But **there is at least one thing we can do about it**. We can stop buying books from that certain on-line bookseller. You know perfectly well who I'm talking about. It is not e-book sales that are hurting bookstores. It is the people who walk into a bookstore, listen to the recommendations of the knowledgeable people who work there, find books they like, and then proceed to go home and buy those books online. They pay a little less (the way they do for honey produced by companies that regularly medicate their bees). But most people have no clue what's happening behind the bookselling scenes, the same way most people don't know how honey is produced and mass marketed.

Let me tell you something that most people don't know about that A company. Most bookstore owners won't tell you, because if they do, it sounds like they're bad-mouthing the competition. Complaining leaves a bad taste in the mouths of many people. Well, today I'm not complaining. I'm stating facts.

When you buy a book from a bookstore, **the bookstore gets 40%.** Out of that, they have to pay their overhead (salaries, rent, the cost of shipping books in or out, and so on). The 60% that goes to the publisher (and which the bookstore has **already paid** to that publisher) gets divided between the publisher's overhead and, at the bottom of the list, the author. On hard-cover books, depending on who the publisher is, the author may get as much as $5. On trade paperbacks, maybe a dollar or two. On the mass-market paperbacks, usually around a quarter or maybe 30 cents.

Amazon, on the other hand, takes a cut of 55%. And they never pay anything for shipping. The publisher is never reimbursed for shipping costs when they send books that Amazon orders, and you know darn well that **you** pay for the shipping when Amazon sends books to you. Publishers, with their fixed costs of doing business (salaries, office costs, printing prices, and so on) have to make do on that 45% they receive. And the author's royalties are proportionally lower as a result.

My father always told me, "You get what you pay for." When we buy cheap, we get cheap. With honey we can taste the difference. With books, we may not realize what we've done until our favorite bookstore closes its doors.

The people who used to kill whales gradually found different lines of work when the U.S. put a moratorium on the use of whale products in this country. The bee industry is eventually going to have to change too. And I certainly hope that independent bookstores are still around when my grandchildren have grandkids of their own.

We can make a difference. I'm just so sorry it's too late to save Cowan's Book Nook.

BeeAttitude for Day #274: *Blessed are those who eat good honey, for they shall glow with goodness from their tummies.*

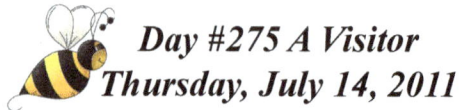
Day #275 A Visitor
Thursday, July 14, 2011

A friend of mine sent me a photo she'd taken just a day or two ago.

© 2011 Linda Yeager Scott

Someone came to visit her.

Or rather, to visit her roses.

I think I like my bees better.

They don›t *eat* the flowers.

BeeAttitude for Day #275: *Blessed are those who plant lots of extras, for they shall still have some left over at the end.*

Day #276 To Feed or Not to Feed - That is the Question Friday, July 15, 2011

Here I go again, wondering whether I should give my girls some extra food.

I've cooked up a 1 to 1 sugar/water mixture by weight (boil a pint of water, add two cups of sugar – at least I hope those are the right measurements), and it's cooling on the windowsill as I write this.

I took an old goat-milk jug and added a stick (so the bees can walk down to the sugar mixture). I wrapped a loop of wire around the handle so I can hang it from a hook underneath the overhang (so it won't get rained on and diluted).

Now, do I put it out there or not? Do I feed the girls or let them tough it out on their own?

Do I really believe in all this stuff I've been preaching about a totally natural approach to beekeeping? Mama Nature may provide, but when people clear-cut the land for subdivisions, Mama gets left out sometimes. You'd be surprised at how few of my neighbors have any flowers whatsoever in their yards. **My yard looks like an OASIS (or a jungle if you're feeling less open-minded)** compared to theirs. But I fully understand that my yard alone can't support 60,000 bees.

So, do I let Mama Nature thin their ranks? Or, once the sugar syrup has cooled enough, do I cave in and feed them?

Wish I knew the answer.

BeeAttitude for Day #276: *Blessed are those who let people on crutches cut in front of them in line, for they shall (if they're ever on crutches themselves) receive the same treatment. We are so glad we bees never need those things!*

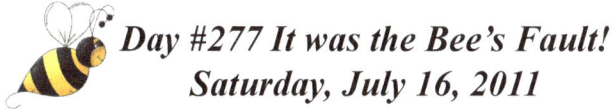 Day #277 *It was the Bee's Fault!* Saturday, July 16, 2011

About ten days ago I fell. Dumb move. Tripped over my own feet. And it all started with a wet bee.

I happened to be standing at the bay window when a huge bolt of lightning initiated a downpour that pelted the hives. One little bee, standing on top, right on the edge, fell – PLOP – onto the deck. I could see her struggling to right herself, but with wet wings she was pretty much stuck.

I threw on my Wellies – I'd just bought them less than two weeks ago at Gunter Hardware, a great store in Lawrenceville that I've been driving by for years, but had never stopped in. When I did, AHA! Wellington boots (Boss brand made in the USA, so selling for $17 instead of the $80+ British Wellies I'd seen online).

Anyway, I stepped into my Wellies, went out with a huge umbrella and a small stiff piece of paper, scooped up the bee, deposited her right at her front door, at which point she shook herself and walked on inside. "That's where I should be," I thought, as the thunder rumbled. "Inside."

Once there, I opened the umbrella and set it to dry next to the front door, got halfway out of one boot, and began to lose my balance. The Wellies have such good traction, I couldn't shuffle my other foot to get it underneath me. I fell, twisting to one side to avoid getting an umbrella spine in my eyeball.

My left leg lost.

Years ago, when I lived in Vermont, I was struck by a rock (another long story—sometime I may tell you about it) and ended up with a hairline crack (also called a greenstick fracture). This felt pretty much the same.

There's nothing much one can do for a greenstick—ice it, elevate it, don't put too much pressure on it, let it heal.

So that's what I did, after—I must admit—having howled in pain for a while on my living room floor.

My daughter brought me some crutches—she works at the Hope Clinic in Lawrenceville—and I've been hobbling around ever since.

I think another day or two at the most should do it.

It'll be good to get back to the land of the fully mobile. And when I do, I'm going to go have a talk with that bee. "Next time you hear thunder, go inside immediately!"

BeeAttitude for Day #277: *Blessed are those who rescue us, for they shall have good stories to tell.*

BeesKnees #3: A Beekeeping Memoir

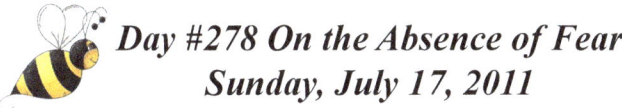 ## Day #278 On the Absence of Fear
Sunday, July 17, 2011

Remember when I told you about the energy-saving film I put on my front windows?

Aside from the wonderful way it cuts the heat from the morning sunshine, there's been another major benefit. I don't scare the birds!

I never realized how much I used to frighten them **until all of a sudden I didn't anymore**. I can stand three inches from the glass (or even closer) and watch my cheeping, preening, eating, singing feathered friends without their being aware of me. They can't see into my living room.

At times I've counted 20 goldfinches on my front porch feeder. Friday morning two Carolina wrens were starting a new nest in a basket on the porch railing. **They didn't know I was watching them, so they just went on doing their birdy things.**

When I first moved to Atlanta almost 20 years ago, I met a woman who mentioned that her husband was a cross-dresser. He agreed to talk with me about what it was like, and he told me of a most interesting discovery.

Before he'd gotten married, he was dressed up once, waiting for a ride to a party. He was standing near the door of his apartment building on a downtown Atlanta street; it was late at night *("It takes me HOURS to get ready. How do you women do it so quickly?" he'd said. "For one thing," I answered him, "I don't have to shave before putting on makeup.")* While he waited, a lone woman walked down the sidewalk toward him. She walked past him. She kept going. And that was when he had his **ah-ha! moment.**

He had never noticed the fear before until he saw the absence of fear. That woman had thought she was walking past another woman. She didn't pull her purse closer to her body. She didn't hold her keys in a defensive posture. She didn't move farther toward the street. She just walked past. No fear. No getting ready just in case.

The birds are the same way. I'd never before noticed how much I worried them until all of a sudden I wasn't worrying them. **What I see now when I look out my energy-filmed windows is an *absence* of fear.**

Of course, all I have to do is open the door to get back to that old way of seeing things.

Bees are MUCH easier. They never get startled—ever. I don't have to ease the back door open. I don't have to creep up on their hives. I can just relax and BEE me.

BeeAttitude for Day #278: *Blessed are those who are open to learning new ways of appreciating us bees, for they shall relax more around us.*

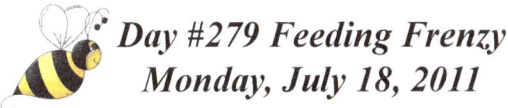 Day #279 Feeding Frenzy
Monday, July 18, 2011

I had absolutely no idea these bees could descend on a half-gallon jug and deplete it within moments.

I went out to the mailbox and heard the sound of a far-away chainsaw... or so I thought. It was actually the sound of a kazillion bees feasting on that sugar water I'd put out for them.

And to think I'd wondered if they'd be able to find it. HA!

Now I don't dare put any more out there because I have some visitors coming tomorrow, and the bees are FILLING the air around this milk jug. Which means they are zipping along the walkway—right where my guests will be walking. But where can I move the feeding station to?

Who knew the world of beekeeping could be so fraught with difficult decisions?

BeeAttitude for Day #279: *Blessed are those who draw maps, for they shall live in a world full of direction!*

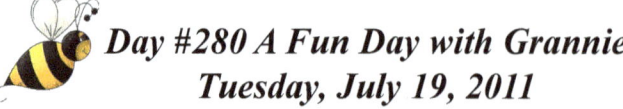 Day #280 A Fun Day with Grannie
Tuesday, July 19, 2011

When you used to visit your grandmother years ago, I'll bet you made cookies together, right? Or, if your grandma is of more recent vintage, maybe she took you to a water park.

And when you have grandchildren of your own, you'll do the same for them, right?

Guess what my grandchildren and I did this past Monday? We were driving home from the grocery store (I'd run out of a couple of vital ingredients) when we drove past a dead deer.

Like any good grandma, I said, "Do you two want to stop and see some maggots?"

You see, I'm in the process of writing the sixth book in my Biscuit McKee mystery series, and there's a body in there that doesn't get discovered for a few days. I've been wondering—as I wrote about the smell wafting over a back yard on a gentle breeze—whether or not I was getting it right.

The deer certainly gave us the answers. I am NOT going to share the photos I took. Suffice it to say that we learned a lot, and here are some of our conclusions. Please put your EEEWW response on hold. This is science at its most elemental:

- Time of death can be determined by the age of maggots on the corpse. There were lots of crawlies, and the man who lived nearby confirmed the deer was killed by a car last Tuesday.

- Smell is almost indistinguishable when we stand upwind.

- Smell is pretty awful when we stand downwind. *Therefore, we stood mostly upwind!*

- A neck bent that far back and around is most certainly broken.

- The grayish brown stain in the grass beside the body showed that the deer had been moved after death.

There were a bunch of other conclusions we came to, having to do with various internal organs, but I won't relate those since there's a good chance you've just finished eating breakfast. I will say, though, that we decided that coyotes and dogs and turkey vultures and possums and raccoons are simply doing their job as part of a very necessary natural cleanup crew. They are eating for survival. The very worst predator on the face of this planet, however, came upon this body and...

- Cut off the antlers and threw the body back in the ditch. (Hence the brownish stain left where the body had originally been when it died.)

- These predators decimated the deer's natural habitat to begin with, and one of them smashed the deer with a moving vehicle.

The animal control facility in Gwinnett County has only three vehicles for the entire county, so dead animals frequently have to lie there for days before they're disposed of. This just means there will be more chances for me to play the role of Good Grannie!

BeeAttitude for Day #280: *Blessed are those who explore new ways of looking at life (and death), for their horizons shall be endlessly widened.*

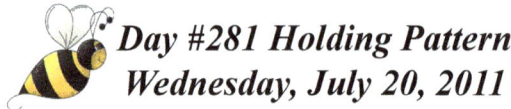 Day #281 Holding Pattern
Wednesday, July 20, 2011

I'm in a holding pattern. Tommy couldn't get by on Tuesday to check the hives, and I'm scared silly of squashing all sorts of bees if I try to open them up myself. The combs are stretched across between the frames – I know that from the last time I opened the hives a couple of weeks ago, and I'm sure it's even worse now.

So—I feel like I really need a second set of hands to do this. Guess I'll wait until Friday. I wish I were brave enough to do it on my own…

What this means is that we need another bee joke:

What do you get when you cross a bee with a hairdresser?

BeeAttitude for Day #281: *Blessed are those who are brave enough to try something that is scary but necessary, for they (unlike Frannie) shall feel a sense of accomplishment.*

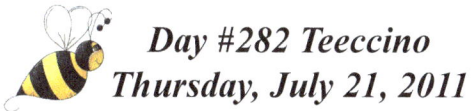 ***Day #282 Teeccino
Thursday, July 21, 2011***

I have to get up pretty early nowadays to be able to enjoy a cup of tea on the back deck near the bees. The later I wait, the muggier it gets. By 7:00 or so it's not worth it to try to relax outside.

I've always been a tea drinker. Hot tea any time of year. The British believe that drinking hot tea at the height of summer opens one's pores and therefore cools one off. I suppose that's true if the humidity is in the 40 or 50 percent range. But when it's 97%, nothing much cools off, particularly when the temperature is in the 90s.

A couple of months ago I went to Grains 'n' More to pick up some food I'd ordered. This is the most amazing company. The owners, Dan and Fran, had been looking for a good source of bulk organic grains. They couldn't get them easily and affordably, so they started their own company.

[2019 Note: They went out of business due to insufficient orders. Yes, their products were more expensive than those in the big box stores, but they tasted better, were fresher, were organic, and were packaged with love.]

While I was there, Fran (that Fran, not this Fran) asked if I'd ever tried Teeccino, an organic herbal coffee. "I'm not a coffee-drinker," I said.

"Give it a try," she said. "It may change your life."

I bought the Almond Amaretto blend. Yummy in the tummy! It changed my life. I am now a committed Teeccino-drinker. And at 5:30 in the morning, it opens my pores for sure.

BeeAttitude for Day #282: *Blessed are those who follow their dreams, for they shall find exciting new directions in life.*

Day #283 The Latest Bee Joke Answers
Friday, July 22, 2011

Well, three people sent in answers, two from Texas and one from here in Georgia.

The question was "What do you get when you cross a **bee** with a **hairdresser**?"

Petie from Texas: A Honey of a Comb-out

Billy, also from Texas: A store-sign that says *"We Specialize in Beehives"*

Marni from Georgia: Buzz-cuts for Men & Beehives for Women

BeeAttitude for Day #283: *Blessed are those (like Frannie) who have leaky rain barrels, for they shall get to watch us playing in the dribble.*

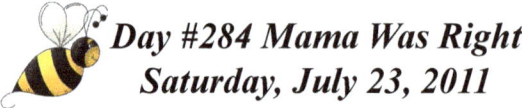
Day #284 Mama Was Right
Saturday, July 23, 2011

Don't you love it (or hate it as the case may be) when one of those pithy sayings your mother was always coming out with turns out to be true?

The latest one for me is ***The hurrier I go, the behinder I get.***

She was right, doggone it. This all has to do with **why bees are easier than other critters.** Yesterday morning I'd just finished cleaning out the litter boxes and I was scurrying to put out the squirrel-proof (HA!) birdfeeders. I've been taking them in each night after dark to foil the possum who is very clever about getting around the squirrel-proof (so far) baffle on the pole. Then I put them out each dawn. Nowhere, by the way, did the squirrel-proof feeder advertisement claim to be possum-proof. There's enough spilled seed on the ground for my resident possum to eat her fill from the mess the birds leave.

Now, I don't really mind possums. In fact, I think they're amazing creatures. **Did you know that possums never get rabies?** I learned that from a woman whose big and downright scary dogs mauled a possum in her fenced-in back yard one Friday just before she left to attend a weekend class. She quickly called a vet to see if she had to bring the dogs in to get rabies shots. The vet is the one who told her that possums can't get rabies, so her dogs weren't in any danger. Of course, the vet strongly recommended that she bring them in for the shots in case they ever ran into a rabid raccoon.

When she finally got out to the car (I'd waited there, having heard stories of her dogs before this), we took off for Tennessee. It wasn't until we were on our way back, two days later, that I asked, "What did you do with the possum?"

"I threw it in the garbage bin," she said. "It was dead. I hope it's not too stinky when I get back."

I cleared my throat. "Denise, haven't you ever heard the term *playing possum*?"

Turns out that possum had been thoroughly enjoying a regular feast in the garbage can. As soon as Denise opened the garage door (the bin was tipped over and garbage was EVERYWHERE!), the possum scooted out. I could have sworn I heard that critter say *thank you, ma'am!* over his/her shoulder as he/she ran around the corner of the house.

Anyway, to get back to my point, I was scurrying to fill the feeders (the hurrier I go) and I misjudged the angle of where I was pouring the seed. Hit the edge of the feeder with the scoop and ended up with (the behinder I get) this mess.

Bees are easier. All I do is plant shrubs and flowers.

BeeAttitude for Day #284: *Blessed are those who learn from those who go before them, for they shall avoid many mistakes. Or maybe not. You folks are human, after all.*

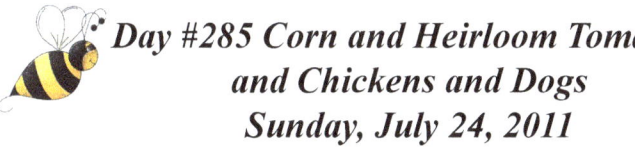 Day #285 Corn and Heirloom Tomatoes and Chickens and Dogs
Sunday, July 24, 2011

Saturday I went to the farmer's market in Lawrenceville as early as I could. The heat index was 102 degrees, and even that early I wilted. But when I came home with fresh-picked corn and heirloom Cherokee tomatoes, and a whole bunch of other stuff (like homemade treats for my two grand-dogs), I decided it was worth it.

Corn on the cob for lunch is my idea of heaven.

But the coolest thing about a farmer's market, besides the food, is the conversations. One of the couples there live not too far from me, and they've invited me over to meet their **chickens**. I admitted to them that I was afraid of chickens (I'll have to tell you my chicken story sometime), and Julie said they had the nicest chickens in the world. We'll see about that. I'll be sure to take pictures and share the adventure with you.

Now, why do I need to visit chickens? Well, in the book I'm writing, the sixth in my Biscuit McKee mystery series, **Bob gets some beehives…**

Why are you not surprised about that?

… and Maggie, Biscuit's nearby neighbor, tries to convince Biscuit that Elmyra, her lead hen (whom Biscuit privately calls Vampirah) is not out to get her.

I can research the getting-beehives-for-the-first-time just fine (by simply reading my own blog!), but the chickens I thought I needed some help with.

And of course, I spoke to everyone who had a dog there at the market, telling them that **WAG** (the **Walton Animal Group**) would be running a raffle soon. The winner gets their dog in my book, and WAG will get all the proceeds of the raffle. I had to laugh because I'm writing a generic dog into the manuscript. I'll fill in the details once the winner is announced. But one dog I saw today must have weighed 100 pounds, and another stood about 7" high full grown. I may have to do a lot of re-writing depending on who wins.

I'll let you know when the raffle is up and running.

BeeAttitude for Day #285: *Blessed are those who buy locally from farmers who grow crops that we can gather pollen and nectar from, for they shall all win!*

 ## *Day #286 Blurry Butterfly and Blurry Dogs*
Monday, July 25, 2011

Well, as I was playing with my grand-dogs Sunday morning, I decided to give them one of those homemade treats I bought at the farmer's market. And, I thought, I'll take pictures so I can share them on my blog.

Belle

Max (and Belle leaving with her treat)

Right. Did you ever try to get two dogs to sit still while you take a picture of them with a VERY slow camera?

But I'm going to show you the disastrous photos anyway, including the one of the blurry butterfly who was waiting for me when I drove home. The butterfly herself wasn't blurry, mind you, but I blurried her up really well when I went *click*.

Then, did I open my beehives and check them out? No. I was so busy writing, I didn't even think about the bees until after dark.

Sigh!

BeeAttitude for Day #286: *Blessed are those who don't worry about things like focus, for they shall, as a result, enjoy their blurry days anyway.*

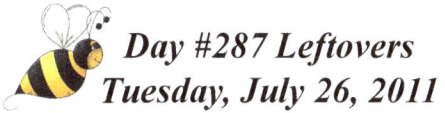 Day #287 Leftovers
Tuesday, July 26, 2011

The bees were cleaning up the leftover hummingbird food this morning when a rainstorm flooded in. They scurried for shelter only to reappear an hour or so later. The feeder had filled considerably with rainwater, but apparently the bees weren't too concerned. They continued to collect the now-much-less-syrupy concoction.

It just means they'll have to work extra hard to evaporate the moisture from it.

BeeAttitude for Day #287: *Blessed are those birds who share their leftovers with us, for we shall join them in happy flight.*

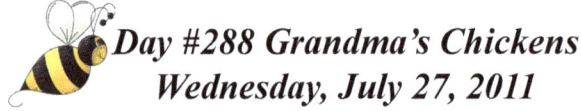Day #288 Grandma's Chickens
Wednesday, July 27, 2011

I think I'm finally brave enough to share my chicken story with you. Please don't laugh at me.

When I was little, maybe five years old, my grandmother, who was a Mississippi farm wife, told me to go down to the chicken coop and gather her a mess of eggs.

The coop was a ghastly, ammonia-saturated hellhole, very different from the houses of chickens who are raised with love and tender care. There wasn't anything tender about Grandma. She raised chickens for their eggs and, on Sundays mostly, for their meat. I can remember her wringing their necks, an activity that generally sent me scurrying to hide in the woodshed with the kittens of whatever barn cat happened to be feeding the gene pool at the time.

The coop was raised off the ground two or three steps. Inside the creaky door were rows of nesting boxes in a series of tiers. The only tier I could reach was the bottom one, but Grandma had said there were plenty of eggs close down.

Did I tell you my grandmother was seventeen and a half feet tall? When she went in the chicken coop, all she had to do was glare down on those hens, push them aside, grab their eggs, and leave.

I was less than four feet tall, which put my head BELOW the level of those mama hens on their nests. I reached up to try to put my hand under the first hen. PECK! I withdrew my hand and tried again. PECK! SQUAWK! This time she left blood on my wrist.

"Grandma! I couldn't get any eggs. The hens wouldn't let me."

Muttering under her breath about soft city girls, Grandma set aside the biscuits she was working on, strode down to the coop with me in tow, and said, "This is how you do it." One swipe and the hen moved aside, squawking a bit, but somehow not coming up with that bloodthirsty attitude she'd had with me.

I may be 5'7" now, but when I think of chickens, I still see that hooded eye and that rapacious beak coming down from above. Chickens are at least seven feet tall, I know in my heart of hearts, and they're just waiting for me to try something sneaky. I hate to be cowardly, but I know when I've met my match.

BeeAttitude for Day #288: *Blessed are those who recognize their own courage, like beekeepers who willingly open hives filled with thousands of us bees. We have stingers, and that makes beekeepers brave.*

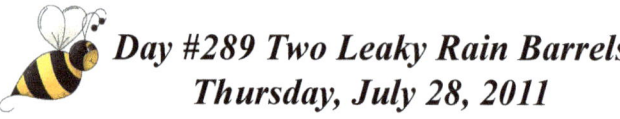
Day #289 Two Leaky Rain Barrels
Thursday, July 28, 2011

The bees are very happy with me, for the simple reason that I've now installed **two leaky rain barrels**. I have no idea what I did wrong—probably the caulking is askew somehow.

My fuzzy girls are delighted, though, as it means they don't have to risk drowning in the birdbath. They just congregate around the faucet and sip away.

I'll try to remember to take a picture some time to share with you, but right now, as I write this, it's 11:30 at night, and my camera has gone to sleep.

I'm up so late because I had to get my latest book ready to go to my three wonderful pre-readers. It's on its way as of a few minutes ago. My pre-readers are the ones who will tell me what I'm missing – *Why is it chicken soup at the top of the page and vegetable beef soup at the bottom?* – important things like that…

BeeAttitude for Day #289: *Blessed are those who walk carefully through the grass, for they shall avoid squashing bees and butterflies.*

BeesKnees #3: A Beekeeping Memoir

Day #290 Why the delay? - and my driver's ed teacher - Friday, July 29, 2011

I went on the computer last night (Thursday) to post this entry – and my WiFi connection wouldn't work. I have no idea what I did, but this morning (after I got the oil changed in my car and bought a new gas cap to the tune of $25 because the one that was on EllieBug when I bought her was the wrong size and apparently I have been leaking gas fumes uncontrollably for the past year)… Anyway, I got on the phone with CLEAR WiFi and a wonderfully patient woman walked me through the process of uninstalling and reinstalling my CLEAR. Now it works! Now I can get caught up. So, here's what I wrote last night that you should have been able to read right after your breakfast this morning. Sorry for the delay.

I was backing out of my garage yesterday, hoping that the bees taking sips of water from my leaky rain barrel would see me coming and get out of the way. So far, I think they've been pretty good about that. I haven't seen any flattened bees in my driveway.

People could learn something from the bees.

A friend of mine was in a car accident recently. She was exiting from a grocery store parking lot, trying to turn left. Nothing was coming from the right. Several cars and a big SUV approached from her left. She waited for the cars to pass her. The SUV put on its turn signal, indicating it was ready to turn into the parking lot. Things were still clear on the right. The SUV did, in fact start its turn, at which point my friend pulled out and was rammed by the little car that had been tucked, unseen, behind the SUV.

She hadn't seen the little car, and the driver of the little car didn't see her. They both would have had a better day if they'd had my Driver's Ed teacher at Wasson High School **WAY BACK WHEN.**

He used to say we had to drive ***constantly guarding against the impossibilities***—the car, the fallen tree, the person walking off the pavement.

-There can't be a car behind that SUV. I would have seen it way down the road.

-So what if I can't see my way around this bend? There's probably not a pedestrian there (or a stalled vehicle, or a boulder, or a fallen tree . . .)

Bees learning to drive, uh, I mean *fly,* would have to careful about saying:

-There can't be an enormous metal monster coming out of that cavern; we would have heard it before now.

The good news is that my friend is healing nicely. Her wrist is not broken; the bruises are lessening; and she had insurance. Her car is not healing nicely, but it could have been a lot worse.

Bumper Sticker: **"Don't Drive Faster than Your Guardian Angel Can Fly"**

BeeAttitude for Day #290: *Blessed are those who avoid running over us bees, for they shall not have to put up with bee-guts on their tires.*

BeesKnees #3: A Beekeeping Memoir

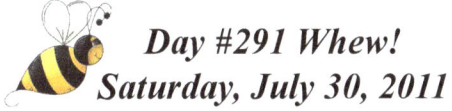 ***Day #291 Whew!***
Saturday, July 30, 2011

Every time I step outside it's like walking into a wave of thick mist. With the relative humidity at 97% or so, I think it would be smart if I'd just hang around—kind of like my fuzzy friends here:

Want to join us?

I'm in the middle there somewhere.

I'm the one without wings.

BeeAttitude for Day #291: *Blessed are those who know how to do practical things, for they shall live a life filled with accomplishment.*

Fran Stewart

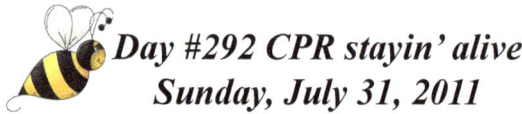
Day #292 CPR stayin' alive
Sunday, July 31, 2011

Well, after the computer fiasco on Friday, I was ready for a good relaxing weekend. Only trouble was, I'd already signed up for a First Aid and CPA course—all day Saturday—put on by the Gwinnett County Police Dept.

Wear comfortable clothes, the instructions said. Well, I could manage that much for sure. If I could live the rest of my life in loose jeans and baggy tee shirts, that would suit me just fine, with maybe a muumuu thrown in for dressy occasions.

I took a CPR course an unconscionably long time ago, and I have to admit that going into class Saturday morning, I was awfully vague about how many times per minute to push. The coolest thing was that the instructor pulled up the Bee Gees singing "Stayin' Alive," and we did our practice with inert practice dummies and jiving music that just happened to be about 100 beats per minute.

♪ Whether you're a brother or whether you're a mother,
♪ You're stayin' alive, stayin' alive, …
♪ Life goin' nowhere, somebody help me, yeah,
♪ I'm stayin' alive…
--*thanks to the BeeGees for these lyrics*

Now, if I'm ever called on to perform CPR, don't be surprised if you hear me singing while I'm saving a life. It sure will help me keep the beat!

BeeAttitude for Day #292: *Blessed are those who teach what they know, for circles of joy shall spread out around them.*

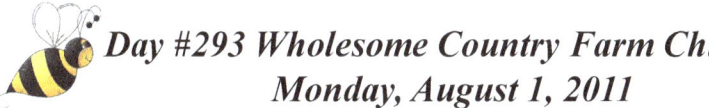 Day #293 Wholesome Country Farm Chickens
Monday, August 1, 2011

I spent Sunday afternoon with Julie Porath at her *Wholesome Country Farm* in Buford GA. What an amazing, enlightening experience.

I've told you about my long-standing fear of my grandma's chickens (see day #288 - 7/27/11). Well, I decided to do something about that fear.

I took this picture of chickens eating at my feet, because I couldn't hold a bird and take a photo at the same time.

Finally Julie took pity on me and my less-than-fancy phone. She took some pictures of me actually holding a sweet little hen (the tiny gray one - 2nd from the right in this photo). As soon as she sends them to me I'll share them with you, but for now I had to spread the good news:

Fran Stewart

I'm not afraid of chickens anymore ! ! !

The funny thing is that **the chickens haven't changed a bit.** They're still just being chickens. I'm the one who had a change of heart—and it's all based on education. I was afraid of those birds when I didn't really know them.

Now that I've met some real live chickens, accompanied by a person who was understanding of my fears, I can see how silly I've been all these years, carrying around a vision of hens as bloodthirsty harridans.

Thanks Julie! You helped me grow a lot. I'll see you at the next farmer's market—and I have a gift of two of my books for you!

And, look what I brought home with me!

Three are white; three are brown; four are light blue; and the two at the far end are pale pink.

BeeAttitude for Day #293: *Blessed are those who help others to grow, for they shall rest in the knowledge that they have made the world a better place.*

Day #294 Scanning Electron Microscopes
Tuesday, August 2, 2011

I found the most amazing group of websites the other day. I've been reading *Beyond the Body Farm* by Dr. Bill Bass, who founded that research facility, and Jon Jefferson, who takes all the stories Dr. Bass has about the Body Farm and turns them into books.

The theme of this particular book was the many ways in which technological inventions have changed the science of forensics in the years since the Body Farm was established. One of the goodies they talked about is the SEM (Scanning Electron Microscope). They can use it to find a minute fragment of metal, for instance, in a tiny cut on a bone to prove that the long-deceased owner of that bone was the victim of a murder.

They also show a lot of COOL bugs! If you Google "scanning electron microscope SEM image gallery," you'll find lots of great choices.

Here's a bee from a fully copyrighted website called MicroAngela (it took me a few minutes to figure out the pun). [*2019 note: The original website I'd linked to on my blog no longer works.*]

I have written permission from Tina (Weatherby) Carvalho to use this incredible image.

Note the hinged antennae. I talked about them last month (June 20th) on Day #240.

Just think, every single one of the 60,000 or so denizens of my back deck hives has this kind of artistry built in. And with a tongue like this, no wonder my fuzzy ladies can gather so much nectar.

Ain't life grand?

BeeAttitude for Day #294: *Blessed are those who like to SEE what they're looking at, for they shall be astounded by the wonder of it all, especially the wonder of us bees.*

Day #295 I Feel Like a Conductor
Wednesday, August 3, 2011

It must be exciting to conduct an orchestra. Raise your hands and all attention is on you. Twirl your baton, and music ensues.

Well, I can do the very same thing with my bees!

This morning as I stood beside the hives, I noticed an interesting leaf on the deck near my right foot. I bent down to pick it up, thereby bringing my head close to the hive. **BUZZZZZZZZ.** The volume and the pitch both went up.

I backed away. **BUZZZ**. Volume and pitch decreased.

Closer – **BUZZZZZZZ.**

Back away – **BUZZZ**

I played like that for longer than was absolutely necessary, but it was so much fun. Eventually, however, the orchestra informed me that they'd gotten tired of this particular rehearsal. One of the members, I think it was the first violin, or maybe it was the tuba, head-bumped me.

Okay. Rehearsal ended. Carry on.

I went back inside.

BeeAttitude for Day #295: *Blessed are those who listen to those around them, for they shall benefit from the signals they receive.*

Day #296 The Chicken Pictures I Promised You
Thursday, August 4, 2011

Here's the proof. I really did kiss a chicken and live to tell about it. This is **Lacy**, a little gray hen who actually seems to enjoy being held. When I first took her into my arms, I ended up crying. She was so soft. And she made little clucking sounds that I could feel reverberating through her chest, rather like the purrs that come from Daisy and Miss Polly:

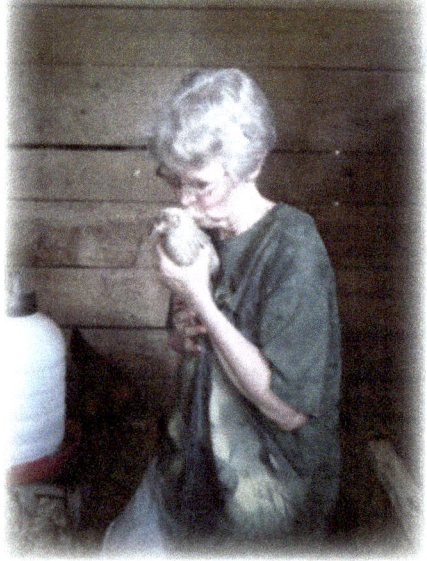

Next we have **Penginie**, the black hen in the photo below. Her feathers had an iridescent green-blue cast to them that was absolutely stunning:

These little ones were in the chicken coop when I first saw them, but Julie and her husband let them out to run around with the big folks. The little ones were curious about being out in the yard, but they kept scurrying back into the safety of the coop.

And, finally, here's Rocky, the fluffy gray and white rooster, and three of the older hens:

It's really fun to watch a hen scratch for bugs. She'll go scratch, scratch, and then hop backwards and lower her head to see what she's come up with. Then she eats the bugs or weed seeds or whatever, steps to the next patch of grass or dirt and repeats the process.

I can't believe I spent so many years so terrified of the idea of chickens. It's good to be over all that nonsense.

Julie Porath was kind enough to send me these photos, and I'm excited to share them with you.

BeeAttitude for Day #296: *Blessed are those who share their enthusiasm with others, for they shall expand the limits of knowledge.*

Fran Stewart

Day #297 The Impact of Little Things
Friday, August 5, 2011

It's amazing what a quart of paint and a bit of elbow grease can do.

Ever since I bought this house (remember – I bought it "as is" seven years ago), my dining and living rooms have sported relatively boring beige paint. The other day I was looking for something in my garage and came across a quart of red paint.

Hmmm…

So, I painted the wall where the bay window is, just that little alcove. Now, when I look out at my bees, I'm surrounded by a warm glow.

Walls to the right and left of it are still boring beige, but look what has brightened up my view! And, of course, Daisy had to get in the picture, too...

BeeAttitude for Day #297: *Blessed are those who dare to follow an impulse, for they shall (sometimes) be highly gratified.*

NOTE FROM FRAN: and if I decide I don't like it, I can always repaint!

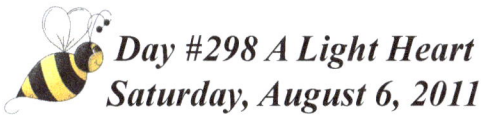
Day #298 A Light Heart
Saturday, August 6, 2011

Time for another light-heart moment:

What's this?
|R|E|A|D|I|N|G|

And this?
WEAR
LONG

And this one?
B   E   E

One more:

O
M.D.
B.S.
Ph.D.

Have fun!

p.s. If you get the third one, I'll bee astonished . . .

BeeAttitude for Day #298: *Blessed are those who laugh out loud a lot, for they shall tickle their own funny bones.*

Day #299 Bad News and Good News
Sunday, August 7, 2011

Well, it's official. My hives are a bust. I opened the hives yesterday to see if they'd done any comb-building at all in the upper story (the super), and there was NOTHING.

I'm trying to assume that they are simply biding their time, waiting for the goldenrod to bloom, but I don't see how they'll be able to store enough honey in that one brief season to get them through the winter.

So, I've put out sugar water for the yellow hive. The brown/white hive I think I'll let be, so I'll have two methods to compare.

The really happy news is that I gathered figs from my neighbor's tree (with their permission, of course), and they told me this was the best harvest they've ever had. I'm just willing to bet that all the good pollination my bees provided had something to do with their bumper crop.

BeeAttitude for Day #299: *Blessed are those who plant trees we can pollinate, for they shall be showered with the products of our industry.*

Day #300 Halfway There
Monday, August 8, 2011

When I started this project of blogging about bees (and, as it's turned out, other related topics like chickens) for 600 days, I thought 600 sounded almost insurmountable. I chose that number because it seemed outrageous, and I wanted to challenge myself as a writer in a way I never had before.

And here we are at day #300, halfway there. I say "we" because this is turning out to be a journey I'm not taking alone as evidenced by the emails I receive from readers. It always surprises me, though, when I meet someone, as I did a couple of weeks ago at the Farmer's Market who comments on one of my posts that she enjoyed. "You mean, you're reading it?" was my totally unprofessional response.

She looked at me as if I were absolutely, totally barmy. I wonder if she'll ever read another post…

And now on to other stuff:

I love Recorded Books. I generally listen to them while I'm driving, but sometimes (like when I'm knitting) it's nice to listen in my living room. I recently checked out *Crime and Punishment.* It's the classic story of a young man who murders a cruel pawnbroker and who then bears the intellectual and spiritual crises that follow.

A usual CD book runs maybe 10 or 12 discs. This one is 21 discs! And I'm halfway through #11, so I'm halfway through Dostoevsky's masterpiece. **This seems to be my day for halfwayness.**

I tried reading it years ago, when I was in high school, but I kept getting hung up on those long Russian names and was thoroughly confused. The recording, though, is incredible. I'm caught up in the story and find that I truly care about these characters.

What recorded books have you particularly enjoyed?

Fran Stewart

BeeAttitude for Day #300: *Blessed are those who read, for they shall have unlimited worlds before and inside them.*

www.ingramcontent.com/pod-product-compliance
Lightning Source LLC
Chambersburg PA
CBHW071713020426
42333CB00017B/2245